ADVANCE PRAISE FOR

Creating Waldens

Creating Waldens is a great, fortifying gift. If we are to turn our beautiful but beleaguered planet toward life, we need quickly to learn to think—and even to feel—like an ecosystem ourselves. Following the provocative dialogue in *Creating Waldens* is a powerful way to help us inhabit nature from the inside; a way to help us live within the core wisdom of connectedness and co-creation at the heart of Buddhism and Transcendentalism. From this deep view, we see our own power with new eyes. We can trust nature with new fervor. We become stronger for the challenges of this magnificent time.

—Frances Moore Lappé, author of *Getting a Grip: Clarity, Creativity and Courage in a World Gone Mad* and *Diet for a Small Planet*

In this inspiring dialogue, Ikeda, Bosco, and Myerson reveal the radiance of Emerson and Thoreau's enduring wisdom. Emerson and Thoreau were leading lights of New England Transcendentalism, a profound engagement with nature and humanism that influenced Gandhi and King and that resonates deeply with Nichiren Buddhism. *Creating Waldens* brilliantly celebrates the continued relevance of Emerson and Thoreau to our lives and times.

—Lou Marinoff, author of *The Middle Way: Finding Happiness in a World of Extremes*

Emerson and Thoreau speak powerfully for the necessity of the deeply principled life, and Ikeda, Bosco, and Myerson focus on the relentless self-examination both writers encouraged of all people, not simply in one part of their lives but thoroughly and essentially. For all who seek to integrate theory and practice—knowing that individual action matters tremendously to social justice—this book will offer that much neglected yet essential ingredient to action: thought-provoking inspiration.

—Sarah Wider, Professor of English and Women's Studies, Colgate University

In a series of lively and provocative conversations, Bosco, Myerson, and Ikeda share ideas about Emerson, Thoreau, and other great writers of the American Renaissance whose wisdom has been passed on through the lives and works of Gandhi, King, Makiguchi, and Toda. A clarion call against authoritarianism, *Creating Waldens* inspires us to challenge social evil through courageous acts of nonviolent protest and find joy in harmony with nature and our fellow citizens around the globe.

—Anita Patterson, Associate Professor of English, and Director, American and New England Studies Program, Boston University

Emerson and Thoreau independently examined the same themes of nature and the human pilgrimage as the great Eastern scholars, painters, and poets, and then added an element of their own, the uniquely American celebration of the self. Here, boiled down to a number of enlightened conversations among three scholars, is the essence of the thoughts of these two American writers and the uniquely cross-cultural and curiously contemporary blend of thought and philosophy that they embodied.

—John Hanson Mitchell, author of *Walking Towards Walden: A Pilgrimage in Search of Place*

Creating Waldens

Creating Waldens

An East-West Conversation on the American Renaissance

RONALD A. BOSCO
JOEL MYERSON
DAISAKU IKEDA

Dialogue Path Press
Cambridge, Massachusetts
2009

Published by Dialogue Path Press
Ikeda Center for Peace, Learning, and Dialogue
396 Harvard Street
Cambridge, Massachusetts 02138

Cover design by Perry Lubin
Interior design by Eric Edstam

ISBN: 978-1-887917-07-0

Library of Congress Cataloging-in-Publication Data
Bosco, Ronald A.
    Creating Waldens : an East-West conversation on the American Renaissance /
Ronald A. Bosco, Joel Myerson, Daisaku Ikeda.
        p. cm.
    Includes bibliographical references and index.
    ISBN 978-1-887917-07-0 (alk. paper)
    1. Transcendentalism (New England) 2. Philosophy, Modern. 3. Thoreau, Henry
David, 1817–1862. 4. Emerson, Ralph Waldo, 1803–1882. 5. Whitman, Walt,
1819–1892. I. Myerson, Joel. II. Ikeda, Daisaku. III. Title.
    B905.B67 2009
    810.9'003—dc22

                                                              2009021517

10 9 8 7 6 5 4 3 2

About the Ikeda Center

The Ikeda Center for Peace, Learning, and Dialogue is a nonprofit institute founded by Buddhist thinker and leader Daisaku Ikeda in 1993. Located in Cambridge, Massachusetts, the Center engages diverse scholars, activists, and social innovators in the search for the ideas and solutions that will assist in the peaceful evolution of humanity. Ikeda Center programs include public forums and scholarly seminars that are organized collaboratively and offer a range of perspectives on key issues in global ethics. The Center was originally called the Boston Research Center for the 21st Century, and became the Ikeda Center in 2009.

Dialogue Path Press is the publishing arm of the Center and is dedicated to publishing titles that will foster cross-cultural dialogue and greater human flourishing in the years to come. Prior to the founding of Dialogue Path Press, the Center developed and published books in collaboration with publishers such as Orbis Books, Teachers College Press, and Wisdom Publications. These books, which focus on topics in education and global ethics, have been used in more than 600 college and university courses to date (2009). *Creating Waldens: An East-West Conversation on the American Renaissance* is the first title to be published by Dialogue Path Press.

For more information, visit the Ikeda Center website:
www.ikedacenter.org

Contents

DAISAKU IKEDA

Preface

A new paean to the triumph of the human spirit, the American Renaissance, which emerged in the New World in the mid-nineteenth century, is an example of how, at great turning points in history, spiritual giants stride forth to break free of the past. The gemlike writings of Ralph Waldo Emerson, Henry David Thoreau, and Walt Whitman—giving succinct expression to the drama of their own lives—have become beloved by people everywhere. Their works constitute a deep spiritual current from which this book attempts to draw universal messages for people living in the twenty-first century.

Two noble, learned, and sincere scholars joined me in these exciting conversations: Ronald A. Bosco and Joel Myerson, both past presidents of the Thoreau Society. Let me take this opportunity to express my respect and gratitude for them both. In addition, I thank all the people who undertook the difficult task of editing and publishing this book.

By way of a preface, I offer the following verses dedicated to the banner-bearers of the American Renaissance, who, through their writings, became cherished friends of my youth.

THE TRIUMPH OF THE HUMAN SPIRIT

Brisk morn in the New World,
the light of dawn
dyes the eastern sky crimson,
brightening endless expanses
of canyon and plain.
The pale mysteries of
obscuring mists
quietly disperse,
revealing the green forest,
its colorful flowers and towering trees—
trees that stretch high into the heavens,
with more than a century of growth,
whose regal bearing speaks of
triumph in struggle after struggle.
Early rising birds dance and sing,
dewdrops on leaves flash gold,
as everything that lives
breathes deep the morning air.

The wind rises to carry off
the fresh energy of growth—
the abundant, vital pulse
arising from these magnificent woods—
transporting it to the clustered skyscrapers,
the very heart of civilization.

Towering timbers of the spirit,
Ralph Waldo Emerson,
Henry David Thoreau,
Walt Whitman—
friends bound by a deep and mutual respect,
Ralph Waldo Emerson,
Henry David Thoreau,

Walt Whitman—
ceaselessly issue the generous
cry of their souls,
a call redolent with the
vastness of nature,
into the endless firmament
of humanity.

Proud banner-bearers of the
American Renaissance!
Before their emergence,
the word *I* never had so proud a ring,
the words *to live* were never spoken
with such earnest dignity and grandeur.

Literature is a clear mirror
reflecting the human heart.
It is only when the right person
gives it voice
that the written word can shine
with its true, original brilliance.

The poetry of these men
was never authoritative revelation
conferred from oracular heights.
Rather, their words were like
treasured swords
forged in the furnace of the soul
day by day, blow by blow,
amidst the onslaughts of
suffering and trial.

It is for just this reason that
they have continued to offer
to so many people—

in different lands
and different times—
the strength and courage to live
when they confront the implacable
challenges of life.

"Camerado! This is no book,
Who touches this, touches a man. . . ."
In these words of Whitman,
fearless poet of the people,
we hear the confidence and pride
that gave birth to
the American Renaissance.

Although they be words on paper,
each phrase and line
earnestly addresses
the innermost being and concern
of every one of us as we face
the unavoidable sufferings
of birth, of aging,
of illness, and of death.

"Nothing at last is sacred
but the integrity of your own mind."
Emerson's declaration of
spiritual independence
resounds like a proud,
solemn cry of triumph,
a paean to the
dignity of humankind.

Having left behind
the distractions of the city,
Thoreau began his life in the woods,

on the pristine shores of Walden Pond:
"Only that day dawns to which we are awake.
There is more day to dawn.
The sun is but a morning star."

It is in the vigorous spirit
of taking on new challenges
that youth has always found
its defining pride and place.

As they grappled with
the realities of their times,
Emerson, Thoreau, and Whitman
never silenced their leonine roar.
The crisp clarity of their call
aroused long-stagnant minds
urging a complacent society
toward vibrant transformation.

Now a century and some decades later,
their courageous call of conviction
still echoes and resounds—
deep, strong, and everlasting.

The workings of nature
are infinite and enduring.
The wisdom that issues
from nature's spring
is likewise limitless.
These great leaders of the
American Renaissance
took untold pleasure
in their dialogues with nature,
drawing from it
the nourishment to live,

the energy to sound
loud alarms for their age.

The word *renaissance* signifies
the radiant triumph of the human spirit,
the full flowering of
the infinite power and potential
of a single individual,
the grand undertaking of constructing
a magnificent sense of self,
a new society.

When the chords of the human heart
resonate with the august tones
of nature's ensemble,
we perform a wondrous symphony of life
whose rhythms vibrate
into eternity.

The same primal laws
permeate the stars that sparkle
in distant constellations
and the inner cosmos
of the individual life;
they are two and yet not two,
indivisibly interwoven . . .

On the azure expanses
of this oceanic renaissance,
the freely intermingling
wind and light
of East and West
generate ever-spreading waves
of harmonious union.

Each form of life
supports all others;
together they weave
the grand web of life.
Thus there really is
no private happiness
for oneself alone,
no sorrow
belonging only to others.

An age in which
all the world's people
enjoy the mutually recognized
dignity of their lives,
savoring days of happiness
in a peaceful society . . .

Such is the world of which
Emerson, Whitman, and Thoreau dreamed.
This is the path humanity must pursue in the
twenty-first century.

Let us set out in quest
of the dawn of a new renaissance,
guided on this
vivid journey of inquiry
by two great American scholars.

Together we advance
in the thrilling adventure
to explore the inner human cosmos,
to find new sources of our creativity,
our planet's fresh dawn!

In Whitman's words:
"Allons! We must not stop here."

Let us press on together,
my friends and companions.
And let us sing songs of praise
to life's beauties and wonders
as we go.

July 3, 2006

In boundless gratitude for the literary training
I received from my mentor,

Daisaku Ikeda

RONALD A. BOSCO

Foreword

The conversations that appear in this volume have their origin in May 2001, when Joel Myerson and I visited Soka University of America in Aliso Viejo, California, just prior to its opening, and then Soka University of Japan and several Soka schools and institutions in and around Tokyo.

All our visits were at the invitation of Daisaku Ikeda, president of the Soka Gakkai International and founder of the Soka schools. President Ikeda's reputation for learning and his lifetime of public advocacy to improve the human condition—by advancing the cause of world peace, championing the preservation of the natural environment with which humankind was originally blessed, and institutionalizing the forms of value-creating education central to the Soka education system—admirably demonstrate his commitment to the humanistic development of a global culture.

Our visit to Tokyo provided us with an opportunity to meet with President Ikeda in both public and private settings; our meetings with him and Mrs. Kaneko Ikeda were warm and intellectually engaging. During one of those meetings, which occurred in a public forum before Soka University students and faculty, President Ikeda asked me what I thought represented the greatest classroom challenge to today's schoolteachers and university professors.

When I replied that I believed it was incumbent upon teachers and professors to restore reverence for poetry and the poetic content of life to all acts of learning, our conversation turned in a direction that neither he nor I could have anticipated.

A practicing poet, President Ikeda, whose writings convey both an impressive lyrical quality, which looks back to the Romantic foundations of his early familiarity with Eastern and Western poetic traditions, and a spiritual and social urgency, which expresses his personal commitment to improving the lives of people far and wide, shared with us his excitement as a young man in postwar Japan at first encountering the poetic sensibility and life-validating lessons of Ralph Waldo Emerson, Henry David Thoreau, and Walt Whitman.

President Ikeda said that first Emerson and Whitman's democratic vision, then Thoreau's spiritual wisdom grounded in nature, inspired the direction in which he wished to move his own life. These influences would work in concert with the heroic example set for him by Tsunesaburo Makiguchi, first Soka Gakkai president and founder of Soka education; the lessons imparted to him by his mentor, Josei Toda, who was Makiguchi's successor; and the life-affirming belief in the individual that he drew from Nichiren Buddhism.

Creating Waldens: An East-West Conversation on the American Renaissance emerged from that exchange. At our parting, President Ikeda invited Dr. Myerson and me to engage in a series of conversations with him on the connection between the poetic heart and reverence for life as represented in the lives and thought of Emerson, Thoreau, Whitman, Makiguchi, and Toda, and in the spiritualism of Nichiren Buddhism. These conversations, which, beginning in 2002, were facilitated by our mutual friend Masao Yokota, then president of the Boston Research Center for the 21st Century (renamed the Ikeda Center for Peace, Learning, and Dialogue in 2009), initially occurred over an eighteen-month period during which we shared our personal and professional histories and discussed the influence that the writers we had selected and the various spiritual beliefs to which we each subscribe have exerted on our individual lives and hearts. Early versions of our conversations appeared in Japanese in *Todai* magazine as they occurred, and then we revisited them again for publication in Japanese as *Utsukushiki seimei—chikyu to ikiru* (Renaissance of Life, Light of Poetic Heart).[1] Our preparation of the present volume has afforded President Ikeda, Dr. Myerson, and me an opportunity to revisit those earlier conversations once more.

And is this not, after all, the truest purpose of conversation? To bring together individuals from various walks of life through *ongoing* conversation so that they may achieve an honest understanding of one another's minds, hearts, and aspirations, and thereby transcend those boundaries of national origin, education, politics, and class that too often separate people from one another rather than join them together as citizens of one human race? Our purpose throughout the conversations now gathered in *Creating Waldens* has never been to persuade one or the other of us to a particular point of view but to share our respective thoughts on the luminaries and sources of spiritual wisdom drawn from the past that have shaped our minds, informed our convictions, and touched our hearts.

Throughout the several-year course of our conversations, we have been cognizant of events unfolding in the world around us as we have addressed our principal subjects. These included joyous events within the Soka community, such as the graduation of the first class of Soka University of America in May 2004, and also heart-wrenching events like the Great Sumatra-Andaman Islands Earthquake that spawned the catastrophic Asian Tsunami in December 2004, the succession of hurricanes that devastated the southern United States throughout the summer of 2005, the disheartening prospects for peace in the Middle East so often reported in worldwide news, and most recently the collapse of global financial markets. Events unfolding in the world around us only reinforced our sense of the timeliness of addressing the particular writers, thinkers, and subjects we had chosen.

With the fulfillment of Makiguchi's pedagogical theories and Toda's educational practices in the preparation and then graduation of that first class from Soka University of America, we witnessed the transcendence of the ideal educational vision championed by these men to shores quite far from that vision's origin. Similarly, against the backdrop of the natural catastrophes, famines, outbreaks of international hostilities, and global economic crises that have occurred over the period of our conversations, we gained a greater appreciation of the connection between the everyday, mid-nineteenth-century concerns of Emerson, Thoreau, and Whitman, and the intellectual and ethical needs of our own time.

With Whitman, for instance, we could affirm that the poetic vision of the oneness of all humanity he voiced in his ecstatic claim in "Song of Myself" is as valid today as when he first published these lines in 1855:

> I celebrate myself, and sing myself,
> And what I assume you shall assume,
> For every atom belonging to me as good belongs to you.[2]

In the confluence of natural disasters with climatic changes such as global warming that are laying waste to so much of our world's environment, we could similarly affirm that Thoreau's principal doctrine—"Nature is full of genius, full of the divinity"—which he expressed in his journal on January 5, 1856,[3] is a conviction that humankind would do well to embrace once again today. And even as we addressed disheartening aspects of world events, we could take comfort in Emerson's insistence that, as he wrote to his friend Thomas Carlyle on June 30, 1840, the human mind and spirit possess the capacity to be "poetic," not just "stupid."[4]

During our conversations, we took note of humankind's disposition to sometimes opt for the "stupid," but along with President Ikeda, Dr. Myerson and I have consistently opted for the sanctity of life and the centrality of the poetic heart in all human endeavors. In doing so, especially through the dialogic process in which we have engaged, the three of us have emulated a pattern of discourse, friendship, and mentoring that was common to the principal figures we discuss in this volume.

Throughout their lives, Emerson, Thoreau, and Whitman, along with many others of their generation, most prized relationships established on spoken and epistolary words. They often communicated with one another better in conversation and through personal letters than through their public writings.

In the case of Emerson, Thoreau, and the Concord, Massachusetts, circle to which they belonged—which over the years included Margaret Fuller, Bronson Alcott, and Nathaniel Hawthorne, among others—it was not unusual for letters and personal journals to be exchanged in round-robin fashion as written extensions of the desire of each individual to share openly with the others his or her most intimate thoughts and ambitions. Through the conversation, friendship, and intellectual rigor of their intimates, these American writers found—to use Emerson's term—their "infinitude" as private persons[5] nurtured, tested, and informed by flesh-and-blood relations and responses to their individual thought. And the benefit of such openness was always mutual.

As Emerson wrote in "Uses of Great Men," the opening chapter of his *Representative Men*:

> In every solitude are those who succor our genius, and stimulate us in wonderful manners. There is a power in love to divine another's destiny better than that other can, and, by heroic encouragements, hold him to his task. What has friendship so signal as its sublime attraction to whatever virtue is in us? We will never more think cheaply of ourselves, or of life. We are piqued to some purpose.[6]

This, as President Ikeda explains in the conversations that follow, is a pattern of influence that was not unique to the mid-nineteenth-century American writers we focus upon; it is, indeed, a pattern of influence we also see and many live by today that begins with Makiguchi, extends to Toda, and has as one of its fullest expressions the ideals of Soka education.

Emerson more than once remarked that the highest calling of the poet was to teach his reader to "despise" (by which he meant, to improve upon) the poet's song. Neither Emerson nor Thoreau nor Whitman nor Makiguchi nor Toda ever sought imitators; rather, as Emerson suggests about the calling of his ideal poet, they were mentors—individuals who offered their personal thoughts, dreams, and aspirations for the betterment of humankind and to inform those who might profit from such knowledge by ultimately improving upon the mentor's example.

Throughout these conversations, President Ikeda, Dr. Myerson, and I repeatedly voice our respect for those persons who have been our intellectual and spiritual mentors, but we also acknowledge that our task in this life is not to replicate either their lives or their respective worlds but to build a better world for ourselves and our fellow human beings. That is why our conversations invariably end on a note of hope—hope for peace, hope that all take inspiration and courage from the divinity that, in Thoreauvian terms, humankind shares with nature, and, especially, hope that the aspirations of young people throughout the world will not be thwarted by age-old demons that still gnaw away at the better impulses of human nature: demons such as self-interest, materialism, and despair.

This, too, is a gesture that I believe we each have inherited from our spiritual and literary forebears. For as we have shared them with one another, we now share our thoughts, aspirations, and hopes for a better world with you, our readers. By addressing you as "our readers," we do not wish to see our words remain on the page only but to encourage your own thoughtful conversations on the topics we address among your friends and associates as well as with us.

Indeed, we never claim to have all—perhaps, even, any—of the answers to the most pressing social, political, or spiritual questions of our time, but we do claim the importance of asking those questions in the expectation that answers will come. Although we share with you here such answers that we each have found for ourselves, our collective disposition is ultimately shaped by Whitman, our ideal poetic mentor, who stated in a passage near the end of "Song of Myself," "You are also asking me questions and I hear you, / I answer that I cannot answer, you must find out for yourself."[7]

In a moving tribute to the power and authority of poetry, President Ikeda wrote that the poet comprehends the "boundless potential" of every individual while making visible the "invisible bonds of life / that unite all human beings."[8] Like the answers to the pressing questions of our time, which everyone must discover for themselves and then act upon, all of us must be open to those opportunities that honest conversation and friendship provide to discover those magisterial yet "invisible bonds of life" that join all humans together. Only by acknowledging those bonds do we begin to realize our boundless potential as individuals and identify the unique contributions we are in a position to make to the global community of which we are a part.

Thus, *Creating Waldens* is not a conclusion that we offer for your consideration; rather, it is our contribution to the beginning of new thoughts and, possibly, resolutions in you—thoughts and resolutions that may build on our own but ideally will eclipse those we arrive at here.

President Ikeda, Dr. Myerson, and I have certainly gained new insights into our world, into ourselves as individuals, and into one another as the friends we have become by virtue of first entering and now twice revisiting these conversations; however, not one of us is prepared to rest content with the ideas or lessons we have either contributed to or taken from this exchange. Instead, as our latest conversations during our preparation of this volume drew to a close, we have each felt somewhat as Thoreau must have on a lovely day in 1853, when he stated that he had not yet reached the top of his real or metaphorical earth. In his journal on March 21 of that year, he remarked:

> It is a genial and reassuring day; the mere warmth of the west wind amounts almost to balminess. The softness of the air mollifies our own dry and congealed substance. I sit down by a wall

to see if I can muse again. . . . We are affected like the earth, and yield to the elemental tenderness; winter breaks up within us; the frost is coming out of me, . . . and thoughts like a freshet pour down unwonted channels. . . . Our experience does not wear upon us. It is seen to be fabulous or symbolical, and the future is worth expecting. Encouraged, I set out once more to climb the mountain of the earth, for my steps are symbolical steps, and in all my walking I have not reached the top of the earth yet.[9]

CONVERSATION ONE

Why Thoreau Now?

THOREAU'S THOUGHT SHINES IN THE TWENTY-FIRST CENTURY

IKEDA: Thoreau was one of the leading figures of the American Renaissance. It is a great honor to take part in these conversations with two leaders of the Thoreau Society. *Walden, or Life in the Woods* (1854), Thoreau's most outstanding work, was published 150 years ago this year (2004). In recent years in Japan, growing concern with environmental issues has stimulated renewed interest in Thoreau, leading to great expectations for our conversations.

BOSCO: The honor is ours.

MYERSON: When we met you for the first time, in May 2001, I had the privilege of bestowing upon you the Thoreau Society's first Honorary Life Membership.

IKEDA: I am grateful for the honor.

BOSCO: At the time of our first meeting, faculty, students, and alumni of Soka University of Japan were celebrating; new generations were inheriting the university's founding spirit. In that celebratory but respectful atmosphere, I immediately felt that you and I, as well as the organizations we represented, were entering upon a productive friendship, and that your personal values and devotion to humanistic principles for the betterment of the human condition coincided in numerous ways with my own.

MYERSON: We are all interested in the intellectual and literary legacies of Thoreau, Emerson, and Whitman. Furthermore, as I am becoming more strongly convinced, we share a mutual dedication to education, efforts at self-improvement, and peace.

IKEDA: Thank you for your kind words. I look forward to learning a great deal from both of you.

Thoreau exerted a strong influence on twentieth-century human rights and environmental movements. His spirit and philosophy are certain to shine even more brightly in the twenty-first century.

Humanity faces many problems today, but Thoreau's philosophy and how he practiced it provide great hope for the future.

BOSCO: Our conversations should not be an academic exercise in the traditional sense; rather, they should provide an opportunity for the three of us to talk across cultural boundaries, which may seem at first glance to separate us, and, by using Thoreau's legacy and influence as our starting point, to inspire readers and raise their awareness.

IKEDA: Thoreau studied at Harvard University, where I have delivered lectures on two occasions (1991 and 1993). I vividly remember the beautiful towns and wonderful natural setting of New England, the cradle of the American Renaissance.

As we embark on these conversations, I think of Thoreau's life at Walden Pond, where he experienced with all his senses the vibrant activities of all living things, and his life in Concord, where he fought against social injustice, fiercely criticizing slavery.

Toward a True Picture of the Man

BOSCO: I can imagine no more appropriate way to extend the vision of the founders of the Thoreau Society and to preserve the legacy of Thoreau than to meet with you, President Ikeda, a person of goodwill with whom I and my fellow Thoreauvians share a devotion to Thoreau's ideals. My enthusiasm for this moment and my optimism that our conversations will reach a wide audience are best conveyed in the subtle prose poetry of one of my favorite passages from Thoreau's journal.

Touched by the vivifying warmth of an early spring day in March of 1853, Thoreau wrote:

> The future is worth expecting. Encouraged, I set out once more to climb the mountain of the earth, for my steps are symbolical steps, and in all my walking I have not reached the top of the earth yet.[1]

IKEDA: Wonderful words. To ceaselessly walk, to ceaselessly work, is most important in life.

Dialogue is also, in a way, painstaking work. It may not always lead to immediate solutions, but it stimulates the mind and the spirit in ways that tap into the source of human wisdom. Repeated dialogue points out the path humanity needs to travel.

Views of Thoreau have changed dramatically in the 140 years since his death. The same figure may be evaluated in different ways in different times and places. It is hard to sum up a human life.

Great people are frequently misunderstood by their contemporaries. Sometimes the great are criticized, abused, and persecuted for never being swayed by the world.

MYERSON: Lives are complicated and multifaceted, and this too makes them hard to evaluate. For instance, Thoreau was a writer, poet, naturalist, individualist, Transcendentalist, and seeker. He was also an abolitionist, a critic of civilization, an inventor, a pencil manufacturer, a citizen of Concord, and a citizen of the world. It is hard to pin down the individual called Thoreau.

IKEDA: Instead of either idolizing or underrating Thoreau, I am seeking a true picture of him. He knew frustration and misunderstanding, but he was strong enough to overcome them.

I am interested in retracing the sincere path he followed to create such a beautiful life and temper such a strong spirit. My hope is that we will arrive at a new view of Thoreau, which we can pass on to future generations.

THOREAU FOR FUTURE GENERATIONS

BOSCO: I have several expectations that I hope our conversations will satisfy. First of all, I hope that all three of us will learn something new from it. Academics in American higher education tend to have a narrow focus; they tend to be heavily invested in their own discipline and in the scholarship current in their discipline. Sometimes they pay little attention to viewpoints other than their own. Personally, then, I look to our exchanges as a way to expand my intellectual and imaginative horizons.

My second expectation comes from my position as Thoreau Society president. While I consider myself a Thoreauvian of long practice and an Emersonian of even longer practice, I do not feel that I am on a mission to convert people to become "believers" in Emerson and Thoreau. Both are persons—especially Thoreau—whose ideas enable and inspire conversation on a broad spectrum. As an intellectual, a person of imagination, an individual who cared immensely about nature and the preservation of the environment, and a person who worried about the effects of war, social injustice, and industrialism on the human condition, Thoreau is a figure from the past whose ideas are as current today as they were a century and a half ago. He therefore avails himself as a focus for exchanges of thought on a great variety of topics. My greatest hope is that, through his biography, his ideas, and his ideals, we will be able to identify the terms under which we and others can learn to speak across our respective cultural boundaries.

MYERSON: The messages we can find in the spiritual heritages of Thoreau and other American Renaissance thinkers have profound significance for people today.

BOSCO: And so, a third expectation that I have for our conversations concerns students—students in Japan, in America, and wherever these conversations may be read. I am mindful of the fact that you, President Ikeda, have devoted the major part of your public life to the development and education of young people. I have witnessed the great effect of this devotion in my visits in 2001 to Soka University and the Soka schools in Japan and to the new Soka University of America—all of which you founded.

I hope that, as we talk about Emerson, Thoreau, or Whitman, we will be underscoring for today's generation of students and young people the importance of respect for the environment, devotion to nature, and adherence to democratic principles for the sake of world peace and comparable values.

IKEDA: Future generations are indeed important. I hope that with your help, this exchange will teach us how to protect the planet in the future and how to overcome the many difficult problems we face as an increasingly global society. I also hope that we can make the fruits of our work known to as many young people as possible.

ONE VOICE BECOMES A GLOBAL CHORUS

BOSCO: I believe that a voice like Thoreau's can awaken in the rising generation that degree of respect for the environment that is so vitally needed now. Let me just remark on "respect for the environment" for a moment, in order to make my point. Whether we are talking about *Walden* or any other of Thoreau's writings, it is important for us to affirm for our younger readers the spiritual as well as the practical worth of Thoreau's unique relationship with his environment.

There is also a definite poetic quality to Thoreau's belief that we would do well to awaken in the imaginations of our younger readers. He expressed that poetic quality in this passage, which he entered in his journal on May 10, 1853:

> He is the richest who has most use for nature as raw material of tropes and symbols with which to describe his life. If these gates of golden willows affect me, they correspond to the beauty and promise of some experience on which I am entering. If I am overflowing with life, am rich in experience for which I lack expression, then nature will be my language full of poetry. . . .[2]

IKEDA: The poet is highly sensitive to nature and receptive to cosmic rhythms.

With a few exceptions, most notably Emerson, practically no one among his contemporaries understood Thoreau's true value. Emerson said in his eulogy for Thoreau, "The country knows not yet, or in the least part, how great a son it has lost."[3]

In the twentieth century, however, Thoreau took his place among the shining stars of American literature. His philosophy has since had a profound influence on world history. The still, small voice he raised in Concord swelled into a global chorus of civic movements, including Gandhi's nonviolent struggle, the anti-Nazi resistance in Europe, Martin Luther King Jr.'s fight for civil rights, Rachel Carson's environmental conservation movement, and the democratization of Eastern Europe.

MYERSON: That is true.

IKEDA: Actions rooted in deep beliefs shine eternally. Thinking of Thoreau and his expanding influence reminds me of Tsunesaburo

Makiguchi, first Soka Gakkai president and founder of Soka education. A wholly original educator, Makiguchi argued that children's happiness should be the foremost aim of education.

He fought against injustice, especially when perpetrated by the authorities. For his opposition to Japanese fascism, he was thrown in prison. He died there in a tiny cell.

Second Soka Gakkai president Josei Toda was imprisoned at the same time as his mentor. When finally freed, he inherited and spread Makiguchi's spirit to the world. (As of May 2009, the SGI's network had extended to 192 countries and territories.)

People in many countries, including the United States, Brazil, Hong Kong, Malaysia, Singapore, and India, are putting Makiguchi's system of Soka education into practice. This shows how the real value of a human life depends on how one's thoughts are carried forward, put into practice, and developed after one's death.

BOSCO: That is why talking about Thoreau today has great significance for the twenty-first century.

CHILDHOOD MEMORIES

IKEDA: Let me ask both of you to share some memories of your youth and describe how you came to research Thoreau.

Dr. Bosco, I understand that your family emigrated from Italy. What part of Italy? What were your parents like?

BOSCO: My parents were Sicilian Americans, and I am of the first generation born in America. In New York, where their families settled, my parents grew up in extended-family households that preserved Old World traditions in the face of New World values. But by the time my sisters and I were born in the 1940s and 1950s, my parents had moved slowly away from Old World traditions as they and their parents, who were for long periods members of the extended family in which I grew up, insisted that my sisters and I assimilate into American culture.

My parents, who worked their way through high school doing various menial jobs, were genuinely hard workers. Although my father eventually went to a small college in upstate New York on a football scholarship, my mother's formal education ended at the twelfth grade.

For all their married life, both of my parents worked full time, my father as a purchasing agent for a government agency and my mother first as a seamstress in New York City and later as a saleswoman for a number of companies.

My grandparents, too, were workers their entire lives. My maternal grandmother was a seamstress, and my paternal grandmother was a short order cook; both of my grandfathers were marble and stone masons.

Where were you born, President Ikeda?

IKEDA: I was born in Tokyo in 1928. Our family business was raising edible seaweed. In Japan, seaweed is widely used as a wrapping for sushi. Seaweed processors were numerous in the Kamata district of Tokyo's Ota Ward, where we lived. The Omori part of this region was a great source of a famous kind of seaweed called *asakusa-nori*. The family business dated back to the Edo period (1603–1867).

MYERSON: Although I was born in Boston—actually in Brookline, a few blocks from where John F. Kennedy was born—my parents moved to Miami when I was eight. I have pleasant memories of my time in Boston: going to Red Sox games, seeing the city, imbibing what even then I recognized as something special in the air.

IKEDA: I visited Kennedy's birthplace in September 1993, when I was in Boston for my second Harvard lecture. Kennedy and I were to have met at one point, but his tragic assassination made that impossible.

As the starting place of American history, Boston has a distinctive and profound mood all its own.

MYERSON: Miami in the 1950s was not like that: There was little sense of history and few cultural institutions, such as theaters or museums. The city was so spread out that it was hard to get around.

I found myself spending my free time watching movies and reading books. My father was the manager of a movie theater, and I saw virtually every film that came out in the 1950s and early 1960s.

EARLY INFLUENCES

IKEDA: Dr. Myerson, what did you learn from your parents?

MYERSON: My father devoted his whole life to his business and inculcated in me a sense of hard work. My mother, as was typical of most women of her generation, put her husband and child ahead of herself.

From my wife, who started as a linguist and now teaches children's literature, I have learned, among many valuable things, the importance of a multicultural view of society.

IKEDA: Your wife must be a fine person. Respect for diversity is essential to the development of a global view.

BOSCO: Both my parents and their parents saw to it that my sisters and I were raised as modern Americans. Although my sisters and I always had to have a job of some sort—I, for example, was working as my grandfathers' "gofer" by the age of twelve, carrying bricks and mortar to them when they were working, and in high school I worked as a gravedigger in a local cemetery—our parents insisted that education was our first priority. Accordingly, in both grammar school and high school I studied all my required subjects and, by the time I went off to college, was well prepared for the study of history, philosophy, and literature—always my favorite subjects.

IKEDA: When I was in elementary school, I took a newspaper route to help with family finances. In 1937, when the Sino-Japanese War broke out, my eldest brother, Ki'ichi, my favorite, was drafted into the army. The following year, when my other two brothers were drafted, life became increasingly difficult at home.

MYERSON: As a youth, I liked to read. My reading was wide-ranging and often driven by my interest in movies. For example, I first read Herman Melville's *Moby-Dick* as a teenager because I enjoyed the movie. (Fortunately, even then I recognized that the book was better.)

Similarly, after seeing the movie version of H. G. Wells's *Invisible Man*, I looked for it in the library. Only after checking it out did I notice the large number of African-American characters who did not appear in the film. I soon realized that Ralph Ellison was not the same author—and this was an entirely different novel with the same title! But I kept on reading, fascinated, and thus discovered one of the great works of American literature before it had been recognized as such by academics.

IKEDA: Your experience suggests an important point. Today, people watch television more than they read. But a much deeper, richer experience is to be found in reading and using one's imagination to fill out the characters of a book.

MYERSON: I agree. Unfortunately, my family background did not encourage reading. My mother had attended Farmington State Normal School in Maine for a few years before withdrawing in order to take care of her sick mother. My father went right into business after graduating high school, although he did attend a few classes at Yale University as part of his Air Force training. I do not remember any books in our house, nor do I remember my parents reading anything except magazines.

IKEDA: The state of society in my youth did not lend itself to calm, reflective reading.

After completing junior high school at fourteen, I started working at the Niigata Ironworks, a munitions plant. As the war grew worse, our militarist indoctrination and drills intensified. Life was all the crueler for me because I suffered from tuberculosis.

In spite of the harsh times, though, some friends and I made time to read and discuss the meaning of life as well as the outlook of the war.

In 1945, when the U.S. bombing became a daily occurrence, my family decided to take refuge with an aunt. No sooner had we moved than a direct hit burned her house to the ground. I dashed about trying to save as many of our possessions as possible. I can still remember the cries of people fleeing the sea of flames.

When he returned from China, Ki'ichi told me the truth: "Daisaku, war's not pretty to talk about. When you come right down to it, it's people killing other people. And it's unforgivable." These words—from the gentlest of my brothers, countering what had been drilled into us as a "just war"—penetrated my young mind.

Dr. Bosco, I understand that your grandfathers objected to your going to college, but that you went anyway with your father's support.

BOSCO: During my senior year in high school, an interesting argument developed in our household over what I would do with my future. My grandfathers thought I should be sent to live with relatives in Sicily, learn the trade of masonry, and eventually return to America with an Italian wife. My father, who usually deferred to my grandfathers' judgment as the elders in the family, was horrified and pointed out with a certain glee that, by proposing this as my future, my grandfathers were themselves violating their own edict that my sisters and I should grow up as modern Americans.

My father asked me what I wanted to do, and when I said I wanted to go to college, he declared the subject of my future closed as a topic of discussion in our household. In the fall of 1963, I left home to attend Fairfield University in Connecticut, which was then a small Jesuit university, where I majored in philosophy.

IKEDA: Your story shows the warmth of your family.

A LIFE BLESSED WITH GOOD ENCOUNTERS

MYERSON: In 1963, I went to the Case Institute of Technology in Cleveland (now Case Western Reserve University), but since I loved literature, after my freshman year I transferred to Tulane University in New Orleans.

I majored in both history and English at Tulane. In literature, I moved toward American literature, particularly that of the nineteenth century. I decided that when I graduated, I would become a college teacher of English because I enjoyed reading and talking about writers and books.

IKEDA: What did you research in graduate school?

MYERSON: I began by studying Hawthorne's works but soon decided to concentrate on the American Renaissance, which lasted from roughly 1830 to 1860. To me, the American Renaissance was where the most important roots of American culture were to be found: the revolt against Puritanism, the establishment of democratic individualism, the questioning of the industrial revolution, and—as I grew more and more tired of living in cities—the growing importance of the natural world as a site to be studied and preserved.

This period embodied real values and ideas applicable to the world in which I lived. Emerson ended up attracting me the most.

IKEDA: At last, you had arrived at Emerson. Encouraged by my mentor, President Toda, I too read Emerson in my youth.

MYERSON: It seemed to me then as now that Emerson asked the hardest questions and engaged me the most in attempting to answer them. I also felt that I could make a contribution.

IKEDA: Coming into contact with fine mentors and colleagues must have been a source of great strength for you.

MYERSON: Dr. Harrison Hayford, a distinguished scholar of Emerson, Hawthorne, and Melville, helped shape my passion for books and for sharing whatever I discover with the profession at large. I share my colleague Matt Bruccoli's sense that "publication is the essential act of scholarship"—that we publish what we know instead of keeping it to ourselves. That has encouraged me to publish more than do most people.

IKEDA: Encounters with great persons or great written works can change our lives. That is why I believe no life is happier than one blessed by such encounters.

CONVERSATION TWO

First Encounters With Emerson and Thoreau

The Vietnam War and the Peace Movement

IKEDA: At your annual meeting in Concord this year (2004), the Thoreau Society marked the 150th anniversary of *Walden* with commemorative ceremonies. Thoreau scholars from many countries took part in significant discussions on *Walden*.

BOSCO: I am happy to say that scholars from across the globe came to appreciate afresh the universality of Thoreau's thought. A new president and secretary of the Society were elected. Dr. Myerson and I are proud to have contributed to the development of the Thoreau Society.

IKEDA: I understand that many young people participated in the meeting. Both of you first encountered Thoreau in your youth. I would love to hear more about your youth and those first encounters.

You both were born in 1945. So your youth was spent in turbulent times that saw the Vietnam War and the Cuban missile
crisis—times that transformed American society. In addition, the
civil rights movement, with leaders like Martin Luther King Jr.
who were influenced by both Thoreau and Gandhi, was a triumph
of nonviolence in the American struggle for human rights.

What memories do you have of those times?

BOSCO: I had grown up in the increasingly comfortable and idealistic atmosphere of the America of the 1950s, which culminated in
the so-called Camelot presidency of Kennedy. But Kennedy was as-
sassinated during my freshman year of college, and, as was true for
so many others of my generation, that event became the defining
moment of my adult life. In an important sense, my generation's
innocence—and America's innocence—came to an end on that
fateful day in Dallas.

IKEDA: I understand that you first read Thoreau's "Civil Disobedience" during those turbulent college days.

BOSCO: When I was a junior in college, I participated in the students' rights movement on my campus. Taking exception to my
activities, the college administration requested a meeting with my
parents. The day before the meeting was to take place, my English
professor assigned "Civil Disobedience" for our next class; that
night, I read Thoreau's essay to great effect, for the next day as the
college president and my parents discussed my behavior, I talked
about Thoreau! I will admit they were not entirely impressed with
the arguments I had appropriated from Thoreau in that essay in
order to assert the rightness of my actions.

By the time I graduated from college in 1967, I had become a
regular at anti-war and peace sit-ins on my campus and elsewhere.
I believed the Vietnam War was unjust not only because I was
never convinced by governmental or military authorities' justifica-
tions for an American presence in Asia, but also because, as that
war claimed the lives of so many young persons of my generation,

the world was deprived of the contributions they stood to make to society.

IKEDA: Nothing is as cruel as war. With this conviction, in December 1964—two months before the explosive escalation of the Vietnam War—I started on my life work, the novel *The Human Revolution*.

In World War II, I lost Ki'ichi. Two years after Japan's defeat, a terse official report finally arrived announcing my brother's death in battle in Burma. Sitting behind my mother when she received the notice, I saw the profound sorrow in her posture. Experiences like these were the start of my peace work, to which I have devoted my life.

EACH CITIZEN MUST BECOME WISE

MYERSON: The Vietnam War seemed to me a futile attempt to prevent the spread of communism, which was feared simply because communist countries were our enemies and not because they had actually attacked us. Like many others, I burned my draft card.

Partly because of the prevailing social situation, I decided that, instead of writing a traditional dissertation focusing on one author, I would deal with a group of authors, the Transcendentalists. For me, they raised questions about the importance of individual conscience. Emerson, Thoreau, Fuller, and others in the Transcendentalist movement believed that institutions that had changed for the worse can only be reformed by self-motivated, right-thinking people—not by violence. Thoreau's concept of passive resistance, or civil disobedience, reflects the belief that war can be stopped only by peaceful dissent, not by violence.

IKEDA: In my 1991 Harvard lecture, "The Age of Soft Power," while touching on Emerson's philosophy, I said that at no time in history have self-regulation and self-control supported by self-motivation been as essential as they are today.

MYERSON: In that lecture, which I read with great interest, you went on to note that the "success of soft power is based on volition."[1] I quite agree with your opinion.

You also warned that a "citizenry without wisdom would fall easy prey to authority with self-serving goals."[2] Similarly, the Transcendentalists recognized the need for an educated citizenry, but a citizenry educated with inner goals, not external ones.

For this reason, many of the Transcendentalists were involved in educational projects, from kindergartens and elementary schools to universities. In addition, they recognized that publishing is especially important to education, for the printed word can reach a huge audience.

IKEDA: My mentor constantly emphasized publishing. Reforming society and the nation depends on each citizen becoming wise and carrying out their human revolution, or personal transformation, Toda taught. Cultivating such a citizenry requires strong interpersonal ties and thorough educational activities, which newspapers and books support.

The Transcendentalists' understanding of this point led them also to emphasize education and publishing. The publication of our own newspaper, the *Seikyo Shimbun*, and numerous books in the postwar period was indispensable to the Soka Gakkai becoming a popular movement.

I am interested to know how your lives progressed from university graduation to becoming specialists in Emerson-Thoreau studies.

EMERSON LEADS TO THOREAU

BOSCO: After receiving a master's degree in philosophy from Purdue, I taught secondary English in Maryland for three years and began a doctorate in English and American literature at the University of Maryland in 1971.

After completing my degrees, I began my career at the State University of New York at Albany, where I have taught American literature ever since.

I have consistently divided my academic time between colonial American history and letters and nineteenth-century American literature. The convergence of my interests in colonial and nineteenth-century American life and letters has been intellectually liberating and enlightening for me, especially because my studies in America's earlier Calvinist culture have enabled me to see the extent to which the writers of the American Renaissance resisted those inherited ideas and creeds.

MYERSON: After obtaining my doctorate from Northwestern University, I was offered a job at the University of South Carolina in 1971. At that time, the English Department had one of the best groups of scholars of American literature in the country—and they were all book collectors, which was of great importance to me.

I had a lot of books; in fact, I began buying many books when I was in junior high school. The modest bookcase given me by my parents filled up, and my desk was overflowing, so I got another couple of bookcases. Then they filled up, and we put shelves up on the walls. I bought even more books in college, quickly expanding from one shelf to a whole bookcase the books I promised to read when I had time.

IKEDA: After the war, I saved what I could from my meager salary to buy books from different periods and countries. That was when I first came into contact with the works of Emerson and Whitman, which became irreplaceable nourishment in my youth. As busy as I was, I was almost always holding a book.

As time passed, my collection eventually numbered in the tens of thousands. Although they were all precious to me, a few years ago I donated seventy thousand volumes to the Soka University Library in Japan, aiming to encourage the students in their reading and study.

BOSCO: I came to Emerson and Thoreau the long way around, and I have to say that I did not always accept Thoreau as a figure necessarily equal to Emerson. I was trained in academic climates that read Emerson as the principal architect of American intellectual culture, and that position alone seemed to me to elevate him above Thoreau. In fact, after my studies in classical philosophy and literature, and after the early years of my career as a scholar of Puritan American culture, I settled on Emerson as the major figure I wished to teach and write about long before I moved on to Thoreau.

IKEDA: I find that surprising. What attracted you to Thoreau?

BOSCO: My ultimate attraction to Thoreau stems from three sources: first, the pleasure I have taken over the past four decades in reading, rereading, and especially teaching Thoreau's *Walden*, "Civil Disobedience," and "Walking," which I believe are the central and ultimately complementary texts of Thoreau's life; second, my resistance to the preponderance of scholarship that in many ways still characterizes him as Emerson's disciple; and third, my growing sense that, while Emerson may have been the principal architect of American intellectual culture and an accomplished theorist of nature, Thoreau married intellect to nature by literally immersing himself in the natural environment.

One of the features of Thoreauvian studies that fascinated me is the way in which Thoreau's life and philosophy have been appropriated by so many different persons and put to the service of so many different—and often contradictory—points of view. There is really no *one* single Thoreau.

Even in his own time, he was a figure who traversed the boundaries of many disciplines and avenues of thought. His ideas appeal to reformers of all stripes: to social and environmental reformers who follow in the tradition of such persons as Gandhi, King, and Carson; to literary historians; and to students of natural history—to name but a few of the groups of individuals who use Thoreau's ideas to shape the ideas and values of their own enterprises.

IKEDA: Thoreau's philosophy exerted a great influence on Japanese philosophy after the Meiji era (1868–1912). Kanzo Uchimura, a Christian pacifist from the Japanese nobility, called Thoreau a "remarkable natural poet" and hoped for the emergence of a comparable Japanese poet.

DID THOREAU SURPASS EMERSON?

MYERSON: It was also through Emerson that I found Thoreau, who asks tough questions similar to Emerson's but with greater emphasis on the natural world. In some ways, I would distinguish between the two by saying that while both deal with the role of the individual within the natural and social worlds, Emerson is more concerned with how—once having made up their minds to be genuine individuals instead of following the crowd—individuals can maintain their sense of selfhood when involved in significant social interactions. But Emerson does not address the natural world as well as Thoreau because for Emerson it is more of a construction of his mind than a real place to be studied with care.

IKEDA: Both of you came to Thoreau through Emerson, though not the same way.

BOSCO: Interestingly, although many individuals now appropriate Thoreau and his legacy, few—very few indeed—ever become his unconditional disciples.

The nature of the relationship between mentor and student obviously has great meaning for all of us. You, President Ikeda, always pay tribute to the inspirational guidance you received from Toda, whose style of mentoring places him in the direct line of intellectual and reformist descent from Makiguchi.

MYERSON: Emerson and Thoreau also attracted me because they shared my innate ideas about the importance of mentors.

BOSCO: Although Emerson's presence and thought initially shaped Thoreau, in thought and action Thoreau quickly outgrew Emerson. This is an important feature of his formation as an independent thinker, which I hope we can discuss later by turning to the nature of mentor-disciple relationships.

IKEDA: It reminds me of something the thirteenth-century Buddhist reformer Nichiren said: If the teacher is compared to indigo, the disciple must become "even bluer than the indigo leaves."[3]

Thoreau did not attract a great deal of attention during his lifetime, but in the twentieth century, many people were drawn to his philosophy.

Today, large numbers of biographies and critical studies of his writings and philosophy have been published. As Dr. Bosco points out, Thoreauvian studies have deepened under the influence of social movements inspired by his ideas and led by the likes of Gandhi, King, and Carson.

Even great philosophers can be buried in the sands of time unless their followers inherit and apply their thoughts to reality. My friend Lawrence Edward Carter Sr., dean of the Martin Luther King Jr. International Chapel at Morehouse University, is someone who is making the fullest use of King's philosophy today.

Similarly, I work hard to find ways to carry on and develop the pacifist and educational philosophies of Makiguchi and Toda. Results of my efforts include: the international Soka schools system in the field of education; the Toda Institute for Global Peace and Policy Research and the Boston Research Center for the 21st Century in the field of peace (renamed the Ikeda Center for Peace, Learning, and Dialogue in 2009); and the Min-On Concert Association in the field of culture.

THOREAU SOCIETY CARRIES ON THE LEGACY

IKEDA: What are the major aims of the Thoreau Society?

BOSCO: Founded in 1941, the Thoreau Society is the oldest American organization of its kind devoted to an American writer. Since its founding, it has adhered to the mission of honoring Thoreau: by stimulating interest in and fostering education about his life, works, and philosophy, and about his place in his world and ours; by coordinating research on his life and writings; by acting as a repository for material relevant to him; and by advocating preservation of "Thoreau country."

The Thoreau Society collaborated with the Walden Woods Project to create the Thoreau Institute at Walden Woods, a research and educational center near Walden Pond. In 2001, the Thoreau Society was designated the official support group of the Walden Pond State Reservation as the Friends of Walden Pond, working with the Massachusetts Department of Conservation and Recreation.

IKEDA: Preserving the Walden Woods and Walden Pond honors Thoreau. Dr. Myerson, how did you become involved with the Thoreau Society?

MYERSON: I joined in graduate school, because I knew the Society was a clearinghouse of sorts for work about Thoreau. I enjoyed attending the annual meetings in Concord because they gave me an opportunity to meet with other folks interested in Thoreau and his writings. Over the years, I served on many committees of the Society and a four-year term as its president. I felt that our Society could better serve Thoreauvian ideals by becoming more involved in environmental issues—especially those related to the destruction of Thoreau's natural habitat—than it had been before.

BOSCO: I consider it a privilege to work on behalf of the Thoreau Society and to see that the ideals of its founders are continued in the present and will be continued in future generations. Thoreau never encouraged disciples, but I believe his legacy is worth preserving well into the future. Through his respect for nature and his determination to improve his own and his fellows' condition through knowing nature, Thoreau offers an endless source of inspiration for today's Americans, indeed for all citizens of the global culture of which we are a part.

IKEDA: The two of you have not only served as presidents of the Thoreau and Emerson societies but also co-authored several books. How did you get to know each other?

BOSCO: Dr. Myerson and I have been friends for more than thirty years, and for almost twenty years we have collaborated on a number of significant scholarly projects. As close friends and collaborators, he and I have come to appreciate the many similarities between our respective views of the legacies of both Emerson and Thoreau.

But we have also come to understand that each of us brings to his view of these figures a sometimes slight, sometimes significant difference of opinion and emphasis. Our differences of opinion and emphasis arise from differences in our family backgrounds and academic training, and from differences in the intellectual and imaginative resources we seek in Emerson and Thoreau. I look forward to these conversations as a chance for us to revisit and reaffirm the ways in which we similarly view the legacies of these two figures and to address aspects of those legacies on which we hold different views.

IKEDA: I, too, look forward to the light you two great authorities will shed on Emerson and Thoreau.

Dawn of a Renaissance

A REVOLUTION OF ENLIGHTENMENT AND THOUGHT

IKEDA: Let's discuss the historical background of the American Renaissance—a revolution of enlightenment and thought. Dr. Myerson, you mentioned that you set out to study this era as a young researcher.

MYERSON: The times of the Puritans and America's founding did not attract me so much.

IKEDA: Emerson and Thoreau lived in a self-confident America. Democratic government was advancing. Industrialization was proceeding apace, the railway network was expanding, and the population was increasing. Hammers building a new society rang out loud and clear across the vast continent. For a quarter of a century, from the 1830s until the Civil War, the nation experienced the apogee of the American Renaissance.

The critic Francis Otto Matthiessen of Harvard later coined this splendid term *American Renaissance*. He sadly fell victim to the madness of McCarthyism. Incidentally, I learned in detail about McCarthyism from my discussions with Linus Pauling, a hero of the pacifist movement.

Between 1850 and 1855, world-famous American literary masterpieces were written: Emerson's *Representative Men*, Hawthorne's *Scarlet Letter*, Melville's *Moby-Dick*, Thoreau's *Walden*, and Whitman's *Leaves of Grass*.

I am greatly attracted to American literature of this period. It is like a newly independent youth setting out alone, with boundless ardor for the struggle, with unbending mettle for the challenge, with a self expanding toward the whole world. How can we explain the emergence of so many great works of literature in so short a period?

BOSCO: Perhaps as a function of my training, I take a long view of the nature of spirituality in the New World and particularly of the brand of spirituality practiced in nineteenth-century America during the period known as the American Renaissance.

As I often say to my students, a characteristic of important cultural transformations and epochs is that they do not occur spontaneously. They have their origin in the convergence of recent and distant events and in the emergence of new people with new ideas with which to respond to both the distant past and the current state of a culture.

The seeds for the development of the American Renaissance in the early nineteenth century were sown two centuries earlier, when first the Pilgrims, then the Puritans, emigrated from England to New England in the 1620s. By the 1630s, the Pilgrims and the Puritans had merged into one political and cultural entity. This was easy for them to do because both groups came to the New World to achieve religious freedom and to make a new and better life for themselves and their children.

IKEDA: The formation of the Anglican Church meant that England was not subject to the full force of the Reformation turmoil sweeping Europe. Persecuted in England, people in search of a purer faith traveled to the New World in hope of building an ideal religious settlement. This was the beginning of America and illustrates how spirituality can be a historical driving force.

In *Cape Cod*, Thoreau praised the Pilgrims for pioneering the nation and serving as forerunners for those who would pioneer on a still grander scale.

BOSCO: In an ironic twist, while seeking their religious freedom, the Puritans—as the political and cultural entity represented by the merger of Pilgrims and Puritans was known—denied religious, political, and civil freedom to those in New England who did not adhere to or accept Calvinist faith.

IKEDA: The New England of their time became an authoritarian theocracy. The powers that be sought to control not only people's social lives but their inner spiritual lives.

Roger Williams, who sharply criticized the Massachusetts Bay Colony and was exiled from it, encouraged his followers to safeguard the truth, endure oppression, and oppose the "bloudy tenent" that persecuted them. Williams's unbending rejection of the intrusion of political power into the realm of faith was later reflected in the American Constitution.

No rights are more important than freedom of faith, thought, and conscience. We must never forget that these are the foundations of the rights for which our forefathers shed their blood.

Makiguchi died in prison for courageously opposing the unification of politics and religion in the form of state-sponsored Shinto. The SGI's starting point is thus the determination to never forget this injustice and to continue the eternal struggle in the name of human rights.

BOSCO: The struggle for religious, intellectual, and imaginative independence among the New World settlers, who would eventually become Americans, served as one of the first—and most formative—seeds of the American Renaissance.

IKEDA: The soaring human spirit cannot forever be suppressed. Suppressors may seem to succeed for a while, but even the strongest, most rigid authority must someday crumble. American theocracy ultimately waned as a free civil society was formed during the eighteenth century.

AMERICANS AS FREE AS THEY OUGHT TO BE

BOSCO: As Puritanism, and the Calvinism out of which it had grown, declined, New Englanders joined other newcomers to the New World in the mid-Atlantic and southern colonies to shape the earliest forms of cosmopolitan culture in America. By the 1760s and 1770s, the spirit of independence—political, economic, personal, and cultural—was fully developed in the American colonies.

IKEDA: Symbolic of his times, Benjamin Franklin was a forerunner in the cosmopolitan trend that introduced to America the ideas of advanced European Enlightenment thinkers like Sir Isaac Newton, John Locke, and Voltaire. The time for independence was ripening.

BOSCO: The American Revolution, which began with skirmishes between British and Patriot troops at Concord and Lexington, Massachusetts, announced the beginning of a major transition in American culture. That transition led to America as a nation independent of the British crown and a nation in which, as J. Hector St. John de Crévecoeur once wrote, individuals were as free as they ought to be.

IKEDA: Crévecoeur, in his classic work of 1782, *Letters from an American Farmer*, wrote, "The American is a new man, who acts upon new principles; he must therefore entertain new ideas and form new opinions."[1] His repeated use of the word *new* suggests the hope and confidence that a new kind of people would build a new kind of world. Crévecoeur early on described America as a melting pot of peoples from many different countries.

BOSCO: In post-Revolutionary, late-eighteenth-century America, individuals from all walks of life "melted" into one national identity. With total faith in and reliance on their own labor, the fecundity of America's land, and the justice of their cause in the eyes of God, they created the political, social, and intellectual conditions that served as the basis for the emergence of the American Renaissance in the early nineteenth century.

IKEDA: Concord, where Thoreau was born, was the focal point.

BOSCO: There is no small coincidence in the fact that, just as the Battle of Concord and Lexington announced the Revolutionary War, so too the new voices of Transcendentalism and Romantic literary and philosophical persuasion, raised in Concord and the larger Boston vicinity in the 1830s, announced another revolution in America. It was the American Renaissance—which I read as a revolution of intellectual and imaginative independence from the past.

IKEDA: In "The American Scholar," Emerson wrote, "Our day of dependence, our long apprenticeship to the learning of other lands, draws to a close."[2] Spiritual and cultural independence is harder to attain than political independence because it requires self-searching, self-refinement, the profoundest introspection to the core of one's being, and the subsequent reconstruction of one's world from its foundations.

Shakyamuni Buddha, who twenty-five-hundred years ago won spiritual independence from the established Indian religions, teaches us, "The supreme victor is not he who wins over a million people on a battlefield but he who triumphs only over himself."

The American Renaissance was a hymn of triumph by the victors in a war of spiritual independence. Its significance extends to all humankind.

An "Original Relation to the Universe"

BOSCO: The great voice of this generation was Emerson's, and his essay *Nature*, which was published in 1836, announced a new doctrine of what it meant to be an American. Although in time Emerson would address a larger audience than his initial and almost exclusively American audience, from 1836 until the early 1840s, in essays such as *Nature*, "The American Scholar," and "Self-Reliance," he was directly addressing those members of the first and second generations born in post-revolutionary America on the means to construct a world of their own that was to be unencumbered by political, social, or theological doctrines inherited from America's distant—either Calvinistic or European—past.

Thoreau, Fuller, Bronson Alcott, and many others of their generation heard in *Nature*'s stirring opening paragraph Emerson's call to "build . . . your own world":[3]

> Our age is retrospective. It builds the sepulchres of the fathers. It writes biographies, histories, and criticism. The foregoing generations beheld God and nature face to face; we, through their eyes. Why should not we also enjoy an original relation to the universe? Why should not we have a poetry and philosophy of insight and not of tradition, and a religion by revelation to us, and not the history of theirs? Embosomed for a season in nature, whose floods of life stream around and through us, and invite us by the powers they supply, to action proportioned to nature, why

should we grope among the dry bones of the past . . . ? The sun shines to-day also. There is more wool and flax in the fields. There are new lands, new men, new thoughts. Let us demand our own works and laws and worship.[4]

IKEDA: I find this passage deeply moving. In *Nature*, which reveals his vision for a new humanism, Emerson wrote that humanity is blessed with a fundamental connection to the universe.

In a similar vein, the Lotus Sutra, the paramount Mahayana Buddhist scripture, teaches that the life of every person, here and now, is capable of opening into the eternal and universal. In other words, a single human life is supremely precious and can expand into unity with the cosmos.

In modern, materialistic society, in which humanity is depleted, such cosmic humanism is most needed to rehabilitate humankind. In harmony with the Lotus Sutra's spirit, Emerson's philosophy can make great contributions to this new humanism.

BOSCO: Although, following Oliver Wendell Holmes, modern scholars and cultural critics have cited Emerson's lecture on "The American Scholar" as America's declaration of intellectual independence, I believe Emerson first made the call for America's intellectual independence in *Nature*.

IKEDA: Emerson specifically discussed American culture in "The American Scholar," but *Nature* projects a more universal vision.

BOSCO: The American Renaissance as we read it today is a complex epoch of American culture. Literarily, in the writings of Emerson, Thoreau, Fuller, Poe, Hawthorne, Melville, Whitman, and so many others, it represents the birth of new forms and a new style of writing in America; it represents, if you will, the end of American writers' dependence upon European literary models.

IKEDA: It was the real birth of American literature.

MYERSON: The American Renaissance may be called the first period in American literary history when authors seriously challenged the values of the world around them.

IKEDA: How does the American Renaissance continue to exert an influence today?

MYERSON: The best ideals of the American Renaissance may be seen in some aspects of contemporary American spirituality. There is a renewed interest in finding a spiritual guide to our lives as technology increasingly takes over roles previously filled by people and as our day-to-day contacts are more frequently with machines than with people. And as technology has tended to make us a faceless society, people are trying to reclaim their individuality by adopting lifestyles outside the norm.

EMERSON, THOREAU, AND THE SGI CHARTER

IKEDA: This suggests that America's pioneer spirit is still in good shape. The American Renaissance was a literary and philosophical movement created by a few enlightened people, and we of the SGI hope to revive this spirituality and bring it to as many ordinary people as possible.

MYERSON: The ways in which organizations such as the SGI are embodying the best of the spirituality of the American Renaissance are impressive. For example, many of the purposes and principles in the SGI Charter reflect these ideals, particularly of Emerson and Thoreau.

IKEDA: Emerson and Thoreau grasped the best of Eastern thought and spread it in American society with vigor. In this sense, they effected a renaissance of Eastern philosophy, too.

The SGI promotes peace, culture, and education based on

Nichiren Buddhism. The Nichiren philosophy of respect for the dignity of life and humanity embodies the Lotus Sutra's essence. The SGI strives to bring this philosophy to all areas of contemporary society.

MYERSON: First, the SGI Charter[5] calls for "respect for the sanctity of life," just as Emerson and Thoreau valued all things in the natural world because of their embodiment of the spirit of God. The Charter's second principle asks that we "safeguard fundamental human rights and not discriminate," a basic tenet of those involved in the antislavery movement.

The third desires "freedom of religion and religious expression," just as the Transcendentalists sought freedom from the yoke of institutionalized religion so that they could practice their own beliefs. The fourth wishes for "grass-roots exchange," much as Emerson and Thoreau lectured and published to reach people at every level of society. Indeed, many of their best friends in Concord were farmers rather than rich townspeople.

The fifth encourages SGI members to "contribute toward the prosperity of their respective societies as good citizens," just as the American Renaissance authors asked their readers to re-evaluate society and their relationship to it. (The sixth regards the autonomy of the SGI's constituent organizations.)

The seventh calls for "respect [for] other religions," just as the Transcendentalists studied the ideas of world religions, and Emerson and Thoreau were involved in making Eastern texts available in America. The eighth promotes "cultural diversity," much as Emerson and Thoreau wanted Westerners to be aware of non-Western cultures, such as those in the Middle East and Asia.

The ninth, with its emphasis on the "protection of nature and the environment," could have been written by Emerson or Thoreau; and the tenth, which encourages education, scholarship, and the enabling of "all people to cultivate their individual character and enjoy fulfilling and happy lives," presents a life goal that would have been endorsed by the Transcendentalists.

IKEDA: I am grateful for your understanding of the aims the SGI is working hard to attain.

Aurelio Peccei, my late friend and founder of the Club of Rome, said some profound things on the need for spiritual revolution. Leaning forward in his chair, he would tell me with great intensity that the human race has experienced three revolutions thus far: the industrial revolution, the scientific revolution, and the technological revolution. All of these were external. The problem was that the wisdom to use the fruits of those revolutions was never developed.

Dr. Peccei would continue that the human race, which possesses an astonishing amount of knowledge, is astonishingly ignorant of how it should behave. Though our technology is developing quickly, our cultural development has stopped and, in fact, petrified. To bridge the gap between the two, Dr. Peccei insisted, we need a renaissance of the human spirit, a revolution in human beings themselves.

We of the SGI strive for human revolution. Without efforts to change human beings themselves, social reformation is impossible. For the sake of a new spiritual renaissance, we must hope for the advent of a new and flourishing American Renaissance.

CONVERSATION FOUR

Refusing "All the Accustomed Paths"

IKEDA: Nothing is more beautiful than burgeoning youth. Young people shine with hope. Being in their presence—their brilliance like the rising sun—cheers me immensely.

Soka University of America held its fourth entrance ceremony this year (2004), attended by smiling young citizens of the world. As the university founder, I am happy that we now have students from thirty-two nations.

BOSCO: Congratulations on witnessing your long-cherished dream come true to bring the transformative power of Soka education to an even wider audience than it has enjoyed thus far.

The beautiful campus of the new Soka University of America is something to behold. Approaching by car, one sees it rising in the distance, a fitting symbol of the impact that Soka education has on the intellect and imagination of the students it serves.

Setting aside the architectural splendor, for me the most impressive aspects of the university are, in fact, found in the intellectual curiosity and imaginative resourcefulness of the new classes of students. They are each year now coming to Soka University of America from all around the world to pursue their education.

Their eagerness in sharing with one another the experiences they have had prior to coming to the university and their openness to new knowledge gained from their exchanges with fellow students, as well as, of course, with their professors, are signs that this is a great university in the making and that already it is serving a noble purpose.

IKEDA: Thank you for your kind words. In his congratulatory address, Jack W. Peltason, former president of the University of California, also praised our wonderful students, who have come to Soka University of America from all over the world to study humanism and broaden their outlook. He stressed the students' delight in engaging in dialogue, respecting others, and studying diverse cultures, never lapsing into narrow nationalism.

This attitude, he added, will help Soka University of America stand out among American universities. We are determined to do our utmost to justify the faith he has put in us.

Dr. Bosco, you delivered a lecture at Soka University of America (in February 2004) and taught a special course on "Nineteenth-century American Literature," which our students found enlightening. Thank you again.

BOSCO: Impressed at Soka University of America by the poetic spirit of your vision, I lectured on the things you have in common with Emerson, Thoreau, and Whitman, emphasizing the ways you each share a philosophy of self-development though poetry.

IKEDA: My case aside, certainly the idea of self-development through poetry was a mainstay in the lives of Emerson, Thoreau, and Whitman.

IKEDA: Thoreau spent almost his entire life in Concord. The name Concord refers to the peaceful negotiations through which the colonists obtained the land from the indigenous people. Of the river flowing through town, Thoreau wrote, "It will be Concord River only while men lead peaceable lives on its banks."[1]

Concord was then a prosperous country town with a population of less than two thousand, mostly farmers. But idealistic intellectuals like Emerson lived there, too, creating a cultural ambience more stimulating than anywhere else in America.

BOSCO: In a journal entry dated December 5, 1856, Thoreau described his life and his delight in having been born in the first half of the nineteenth century and been a citizen of Concord:

> My themes shall not be far-fetched. I will tell of homely every-day phenomena and adventures.... I have never got over my surprise that I should have been born into the most estimable place in all the world, and in the very nick of time, too.[2]

The enthusiasm with which Thoreau described his life as the pursuit of "homely every-day phenomena and adventures" is genuine, as is the sense of joy with which he expressed his belief that he was "born into the most estimable place in all the world, and in the very nick of time."

IKEDA: When Thoreau was born in 1817, the Revolutionary War was a thing of the past, the Civil War yet to come. His youth was spent in a happy place at a happy time.

BOSCO: His biographers have always found it difficult to name him or define his character through conventional pronouncements such as "Thoreau was a...." Over the course of his forty-four years, Thoreau was variously a teacher and tutor; a lecturer on the lyceum circuit; an author and literary naturalist; an abolitionist and political reformer; a philosopher; an environmentalist; a sojourner at Walden Pond; and an explorer of Concord's rivers, the Maine Woods, and Cape Cod. Defining Thoreau's life or character through reference to only one or a combination of only some of these activities does severe disservice to the range of his intellectual interests and imaginative expression, and certainly diminishes the profound impact his life and thought have exerted on American culture—indeed, on global culture—over the century and a half since his death.

IKEDA: Again, it is wrong to reduce any human being—especially a versatile one like Thoreau—to a single characteristic. In many ways, Thoreau's life itself is even more appealing than his written works.

He reminds me of Gandhi, who, when asked what his message was, replied, "My life is my message."[3] Had Thoreau been asked a similar question in his later years, he probably would have had the same response. His entire life was one wonderful literary work.

More Than One Life To Lead

BOSCO: Thoreau's most straightforward explanation for his life and character comes at the conclusion of *Walden*, where he explains his reason for leaving the pond. Believing he had more than one life to lead, he felt he could spare no more time on that one.

IKEDA: Tracing Thoreau's life, one finds new challenges, new discoveries, and new progress at each stage. As Emerson said in his eulogy for his friend, Thoreau refused "all the accustomed paths."[4]

And in *Walden*, he alluded to the Confucian classic *Daxue*, advising that one should renew oneself daily and completely, and go on doing so over and over, never losing enthusiasm.[5] Thoreau's writings are a guide to his struggle to live in the exceptional way he chose.

MYERSON: They record the extraordinary accomplishment of an individual who, to paraphrase his own words, lived deep and sucked out all the marrow of life. *A Week on the Concord and Merrimack Rivers* (1849) recreates an excursion he took with his brother John in 1839; *Walden* reports the insights he gained while living at Walden Pond between July 4, 1845, and September 6, 1847.

IKEDA: These are his only works published during his lifetime.

MYERSON: *The Maine Woods*, published in 1864, two years after his death, recounts his three expeditions to the Maine wilderness between 1838 and 1857. *Cape Cod*, published in 1865, describes his four walking tours across that prized New England landscape between 1849 and 1857.

BOSCO: The fourteen volumes of his journal, which Thoreau began in 1837 at the suggestion of Emerson, preserve the spontaneity, originality, and depth of his observations of and reflections on all that he saw and felt during the twenty-five-year span these volumes record.

IKEDA: In the following lovely verse, Thoreau expressed his eagerness to plumb all life's possibilities: "My life has been the poem I would have writ / But I could not both live and utter it."[6]

All of his philosophy is revealed in his journal, which provided the basis for his essays and lectures.

A PROPHETIC VOICE

BOSCO: A host of essays, many of them drawn from lectures but published only after his death, establish Thoreau as America's premier patriot and social critic, her earliest prophet of the advantages of a life lived wholly in concert with nature, and her most influential proponent for the preservation of the natural environment.

IKEDA: He was ahead of his time in discussing many of the problem areas—the environment, mass culture, human rights, the media—that the whole world is facing today. Indeed, timely observations on all these topics are to be found throughout his work.

Although all his writing is compelling, he is especially brilliant on nature, combining scientific and spiritual observations, high literary and ethical standards, and—most inspiring of all—his love for the natural world and respect for life.

MYERSON: For their blending of science with acute observation, "The Succession of Forest Trees" (1860) and the lyrical "Autumnal Tints" (1862) are two noteworthy examples of his natural-history writings.

IKEDA: He also wrote sharp criticisms on societal contradictions. We find in his works expressions of anger against human arrogance, social evils, and injustice.

BOSCO: He harshly criticized slavery in "Slavery in Massachusetts" (1854) and in "Life Without Principle" (1863). In 1859, he wrote "A Plea for Captain John Brown" in defense of the abolitionist John Brown, who was arrested and hanged for raiding an arsenal and armory.

In these three works, he developed some of his most passionate and sustained arguments against capitalism; the inhumanity of the institution of slavery; the perfidy of governments that suppress individual conscience; and the shame of those who, knowing better, fail to heed the dictates of individual conscience.

IKEDA: In "Slavery in Massachusetts," for example, Thoreau wrote:

> The law will never make men free; it is men who have got to make the law free. They are the lovers of law and order, who observe the law when the government breaks it.[7]

Thoreau, a man to whom contradictions in society were perfectly clear and deserving of criticism, looked down upon political authority from a spiritual height.

BOSCO: *Walden* is unquestionably Thoreau's masterpiece, but had he written no more during his life, "Civil Disobedience" (1849) and "Walking" (1862) would have guaranteed his reputation throughout the ages. "Civil Disobedience" has directly inspired such momentous cultural transformations as the nonviolent revolution led by Gandhi in India; the civil rights movement led by King in the United States; and the global peace movement led by you, President Ikeda.

"Walking," along with *Walden*, has inspired numerous champions of environmentalism, including Rachel Carson, John Muir, Edward Abbey, and Annie Dillard.

THOREAU FIRST ENCOUNTERS EMERSON

IKEDA: Thoreau's works inspire in us the will to live. Beyond being classics, they can inspire today's youth with the courage of this nineteenth-century American idealist. I hope that, inspired by the great lessons of his life, large numbers of twenty-first-century Thoreaus will emerge to smash stereotypes and live their lives freely in their own ways.

After graduating from the Concord Academy at sixteen, Thoreau entered Harvard College. Disliking the emphasis on rote memorization, he spent his time in the library reading on his own. Preferring self-study, he seems to have assimilated naturally the principles Emerson propounds in "Self-Reliance."

BOSCO: Although he received the classical education proper for his time and place at Harvard during the 1830s, it is undeniably the case that his real education took place in the company of Emerson and in the woods, meadows, waterways, and fields surrounding the Concord that Thoreau loved.

IKEDA: Nothing contributes to a young person's growth like encounters with great human beings. Meeting my mentor when I was nineteen is the greatest happiness of my life.

He always told me: "Do everything you can to meet great people, even if you can only listen to them from afar. This is the supreme form of education and a great gift to yourself."

Great people are living models of the possibilities inherent in human life. Association with them stimulates the desire to emulate them and the confidence that you can. A great soul is the greatest inspiration. Such encounters help us develop more than a thousand books would.

Thoreau was twenty when he first met Emerson, in the autumn of 1837, the year he graduated from Harvard.

BOSCO: Since the nineteenth century, scholars have been fascinated by and debated the nature of the relationship between Emerson and Thoreau. Surely, it began as a mentor-student relationship.

In the late 1830s, just as Thoreau was completing his studies at Harvard, he not only read Emerson's *Nature* but also came into close personal contact with this great man. From my viewpoint, that Thoreau developed a close relationship with Emerson makes perfect sense and in no way detracts from the originality of Thoreau's ideas and writing.

IKEDA: Not in the least. Thoreau was always more than Emerson's follower.

BOSCO: Emerson was, after all, Thoreau's elder; he was an extraordinarily well-read and even world-traveled man by the time Thoreau met him. He was the "idea man" for Thoreau's generation; and certainly in the early years of their relationship, Emerson piqued Thoreau's intellect and imagination with ideas and theories that the youthful Thoreau tried to put into practice, like following Emerson's practice of keeping a journal.

IKEDA: While he was acting on Emerson's ideas and theories, Thoreau developed and deepened his own thought. Ultimately, he became a soaring philosopher in his own right.

MYERSON: The concept of a mentor-disciple relationship as regards Emerson and Thoreau is a complicated one. Surely, in the beginning, Thoreau would have responded to Emerson as a mentor, but I think Thoreau would have defined *disciple* as a person in progress.

IKEDA: In "The American Scholar," Emerson said that ideas without action can never become truths bearing mature fruit. Thoreau was better at applying ideas.

His learning from Emerson stimulated enough growth in his own philosophy to startle Emerson. Perhaps this was only natural.

BOSCO: The mentor-disciple relationship that started in the late 1830s grew into deep friendship in the 1840s. Here I think we must distinguish between mentorship—if you will—and friendship.

IKEDA: The relationship grew into one in which the two men learned together. In 1841, when Emerson invited Thoreau to join him in dialogue aimed at growing wiser together, Thoreau moved into the Emerson house, where he took on various domestic tasks.

In a letter to his friend Thomas Carlyle, Emerson described Thoreau as a "noble, manly youth, full of melodies and inventions."[8] He had great respect for Thoreau, whose development delighted him.

BOSCO: By the time Emerson and Thoreau had become friends— throughout the 1840s, that friendship taking the form of Thoreau's temporary membership in Emerson's household and its extended family—Thoreau had moved significantly beyond what Emerson could offer as his mentor.

In his essay on "Experience," Emerson provided us with an important clue as to how that mentor-disciple relationship could easily have ended and been replaced by friendship. Emerson wrote that the world outside his study window—the everyday world of real men and real women—is not the world "*I think.*" This is Emerson's confession of his personal disposition toward theory in preference to practice.

Thoreau, on the other hand, seems to have made a concerted effort to erase any distinction between the world he *thought* and the world he *enjoyed* in the natural environment in and around Concord.

IKEDA: For Emerson, nature was abstract; for Thoreau, it was concrete—to be seen with the eyes, heard with the ears, and touched with the hands. In his journal, Emerson praised Thoreau's use of brilliant images to explain ideas that could have become tedious.

BOSCO: It was not that, having become friends, Emerson and Thoreau had nothing left to learn from each other. The nature of their relationship had undergone a dramatic and fundamental change.

MYERSON: Throughout the 1840s, many people remarked on the physical similarities—particularly of their noses—as well as the intellectual similarities between Emerson and Thoreau. It was almost always assumed that Thoreau borrowed his ideas from Emerson. This eventually began to grate on Thoreau and was no doubt a significant factor in the estrangement the two men felt in the 1850s.

NOBLE EXCHANGES

BOSCO: Thoreau had become his own man and, even by Emerson's admission later in life, had much to teach his former mentor. In his lecture "Country Life," which he first delivered in Boston in 1858,

Emerson, without naming him, revealed his reliance upon Thoreau as his foremost "professor" of nature. In allusion to Thoreau, Emerson wrote that it is better to

> learn the elements of geology, of botany, of ornithology and astronomy by word of mouth from a companion than dully from a book. There is so much, too, which a book cannot teach which an old friend can.[9]

IKEDA: Emerson urged people to learn from nature. Then he found himself in the position of learning a great deal from Thoreau, who himself had learned many things through immersion in nature. Doesn't this reflect Emerson's view of how the mentor-disciple relationship should be?

BOSCO: In his essay "Poetry and Imagination," Emerson states that the highest calling of the poet is to teach his reader to despise the poet's song.[10] By this, he means that we all have the capacity to be poets, but maybe only now and then a great person comes along to inspire and move us to look to our own ability within—and eclipse eventually the poet and the poetry that once inspired us.

This is how I believe Emerson looked at the mentor-disciple relationship generally and how he regarded his relationship with Thoreau specifically. Emerson believed that it was to Thoreau's credit that he moved out from under the shadow of the great man.

IKEDA: A mentor wishes his disciples to go beyond the mentor and develop on their own. In the relationship as it should be, the mentor wants to stimulate his disciples to stride ahead on the strength of their own ideas and actions.

BOSCO: I believe that is exactly what all teachers and mentors should hope for regarding their students. In my case, I have been privileged to have been taught by some of the finest men and women I have ever met.

The natural evolution of the mentor-student relationship has been for the student eventually to move beyond the mentor. All the doctoral candidates I have prepared have been exceedingly fine students. Whatever fields they are working in or whatever they are writing about, they are now serving me as mentors; I am learning much from them that is new to me.

IKEDA: Nothing pleases me more than the development and triumph of young people. That is my major reason for devoting myself to educating youth.

In a deeply moving funeral oration, Emerson, who knew Thoreau's greatness better than anyone, said that his friend's soul was created for the noblest exchanges. In society today, this kind of mentor-disciple relationship—a relationship of noble exchanges— is on the wane. Its weakening lies at the heart of our many youth-related problems.

I am not talking about a unilateral, suppressive, superior-inferior relationship but a creative partnership transcending generational differences. It might be described as progressive comradeship, in which both sides mutually inspire each other while moving toward the shared goal of heightened humanity.

I hope we can give new life to the beautiful bonds of friendship and wonderful interactions of which human beings are capable, as did Emerson and Thoreau in their mentor-disciple relationship.

CONVERSATION FIVE

Thoreau As Social Reformer

Two Years, Two Months, Two Days

IKEDA: A mind open to challenges is beautiful. All his life, Thoreau was aflame with the indomitable will to take up any challenge.

But Thoreau's youth was a series of frustrations. After graduating from Harvard, he eventually found a teaching position but soon quit. After a period without regular employment, he started his own school, but it failed before long. He could establish no reputation as a poet.

A sensitive person, Thoreau likely was troubled by this series of setbacks. Although he must have felt lonely, even desperate, he courageously strove to make his life meaningful.

My mentor always urged us to find the strength to live true to ourselves. Thoreau, who did just that, found the starting point for a new life: In July 1845, at twenty-eight, he moved to Walden Pond, where he would live for two years.

BOSCO: Toward the end of March 1845, he borrowed an axe and walked the mile from Concord Center to the woods on the Concord side of Walden Pond, where he intended to clear a small parcel and build a cabin. The woods belonged to Emerson. Over the next several months, Thoreau finished his ten-by-fifteen-foot dwelling, spending, as he pointed out with a certain degree of Yankee pride, only twenty-eight dollars and twelve-and-a-half cents on the entire project.

He moved in on July 4—America's and, ultimately, Thoreau's own Independence Day. But long before he had comfortably settled into his cabin and the first winds of the winter of 1845–46 had begun to blow, Thoreau found himself having to answer the queries of friends and neighbors about this, his most recent and most radical escape into nature.

IKEDA: In the opening passages of *Walden*, he mentioned "very particular inquiries . . . made by my townsmen concerning my mode of life."[1] They were curious to know why he lazed about doing seemingly peculiar things. There was no way for them to know the nature of the great spiritual revolution taking place deep inside Thoreau.

How did Thoreau react to this gossip?

MYERSON: As he stated in *Walden*, his answer was simple and all the more eloquent and inspiring for its simplicity:

> I went to the woods because I wished to live deliberately, to front only the essential facts of life, and see if I could not learn what it had to teach, and not, when I came to die, discover that I had not lived. I did not wish to live what was not life, . . . nor did I wish to practice resignation. . . . I wanted to live deep and suck out all the marrow of life, to live so sturdily and Spartan-like as to put to rout all that was not life, . . . to drive life into a corner, and reduce it to its lowest terms, and, if it proved to be mean, why then to get the whole and genuine meanness of it, . . . or if it were sublime, to know it by experience. . . .[2]

Thoreau lived at Walden Pond for two years, two months, and two days.

IKEDA: The sincerity of his approach to life comes through in his words. Many people today are not really living life. Thoreau consistently strove to lead a life worth living.

Eight hundred years ago, in *Hojoki*, or "Account of My Hut," the Japanese poet and essayist Kamo no Chomei described his life in a ten-foot-square hut. The title of an early-twentieth-century English translation was *A Japanese Thoreau of the Twelfth Century*, because, like Thoreau, Chomei lived in isolation. But whereas Chomei expressed his dislike for life on Earth, Thoreau delved deep to find the true meaning of living in reality.

Even one day in the forest must have entailed a severe struggle in which Thoreau had to choose between spiritual growth or descent into depravity. Each day was a battle to crush inner evil and awaken inner good.

As he wrote: "Our whole life is startlingly moral. There is never an instant's truce between virtue and vice."[3]

Nichiren also mentioned the ceaseless challenge that true progress entails: "Strengthen your faith day by day and month after month. Should you slacken in your resolve even a bit, devils will take advantage."[4] Human beings discover the truth of life only through this ceaseless spiritual struggle.

BOSCO: When he left the pond, on September 6, 1847, he had completed a two-year cycle of life in which he came to terms with both the meanness and the sublimity of life.

He wrote in *Walden*:

> A lake is the landscape's most beautiful and expressive feature. It is earth's eye; looking into which the beholder measures the depth of his own nature.[5]

At Walden, Thoreau plumbed the depth of human nature. And what he learned ultimately became the subject of his book.

On the one hand, his rustic life at Walden Pond was literally only a short step back and away from the lives of his fellow Concordians—people, he felt, whose physical and spiritual independence had been mortgaged to their lands; to their professions; or to the expectations that convention, family, teachers, government, or church had placed on them. But the freedom of Thoreau's life at Walden Pond cast their lives in stark relief.

Their lives, he decided, were acts of "stereotyped . . . despair"[6] in which they were robbed of their individuality as well as their freedom to choose a way of life for themselves. On the other hand, Thoreau's life at Walden Pond was sublime because it was independent and offered him the chance to identify and indulge his competing instincts toward both a mystic, spiritual life and a primitive, savage one.

IKEDA: Lamentably, without examining their fundamental goals, people often accept mere means as ends. Stubbornly assuming their way of life to be the best, they fail to manifest their true potential.

Thoreau said:

If one advances confidently in the direction of his dreams, and endeavors to live the life which he has imagined, he will meet with a success unexpected in common hours.[7]

His bold experiment at Walden Pond showed that a totally new kind of life was possible. Thoreau was an adventurous pioneer, a social reformer, and a revolutionary.

BETWEEN THE INDIVIDUAL AND NATURE

BOSCO: Thoreau immersed himself in nature for nature's sake, as when he paused to appreciate her beauty and to master the lessons she taught him through the constancy of her rhythms across the seasons and the habits of her animals with whom he shared the woods. By immersing himself in nature, Thoreau elevated his experience to poetry.

IKEDA: From the abundant potential he saw in nature, Thoreau was trying to derive lessons for realizing the unlimited potential of people.

BOSCO: As he confided in his journal, he came to believe that nature offered him an inexhaustible array of luxuries, among which he included standing up to his chin in a hidden swamp for a whole summer's day, scenting the sweet fern, being lulled by the minstrelsy of gnats and mosquitoes, and being cheered by genial conversation with a leopard frog.

In any place and at any time of the year, as long as he was out in nature, Thoreau felt himself expand to an existence as wide as the universe. This confirmed one of his chief articles of faith: "Nature is full of genius, full of divinity."[8]

MYERSON: Thoreau's posture throughout *Walden* represents an extended application of Emerson's theory of the ideal relationship between the individual and nature. In *Nature*, Emerson provided the generation into which Thoreau was born with that one commandment: "Build . . . your own world."[9] The house-building Thoreau began on that cold March day in 1845 was an act of creation analogous to building that new world, and the world he would eventually create at Walden Pond and capture in the poetic prose of *Walden* was a special test of nature's genius and divinity as well as of his own.

IKEDA: So Thoreau demonstrated it was possible to realize a new world based on Emerson's theories. Thoreau's appeal lies in how he derived universal rules from small, individual experiences.

MYERSON: When *Walden* appeared in 1854, the book met with mixed reviews. This was predictable, perhaps, at the mid-point of the nineteenth century, when science, human invention, and industrialism all came together to form a new concept of progress in America.

IKEDA: Thoreau was too far ahead of his time for his contemporaries to understand him.

BOSCO: But in the century and a half since he first took up residence at the pond, Walden the place and *Walden* the book have come to hold dramatically different meanings for several generations. Walden Pond has taken on mythic dimensions that have literally made it seem larger than life. So large has Walden Pond become in the popular imagination that one occasionally hears an audible gasp from those who see it for the first time. "It's much smaller than I imagined," they say somewhat under their breath.

For some of the more than seven-hundred-thousand people who visit it annually and describe their visit as a "pilgrimage," the pond evidently serves as a holy site. And as for *Walden*: It is now possibly the most-read book by an American writer.

IKEDA: Since the book was so unappreciated during his lifetime, Thoreau would be astonished.

MYERSON: *Walden's* meaning and its messages have been appropriated by environmentalists and land preservationists, poets and artists, peace advocates, civil and religious reformers, and most of all those who continue to aspire to Thoreau's ideal life—a life lived "deliberately" or lived as one's authentic self.

IKEDA: The book is a superlative record of living true to oneself.

WAS THOREAU LONELY?

IKEDA: Though he gave the impression of being a misanthrope, Thoreau was blessed with many excellent friends. Among them were Fuller, Hawthorne, Bronson Alcott, his daughter Louisa May Alcott, author of *Little Women*, and her younger sisters.

BOSCO: At Walden, he tested the relative merits of society and solitude and found that both were necessary to complete a human being. We have plenty of evidence from both his journal and external sources of his reliance on people like his brother, John Thoreau, and of his close relationships with Emerson, the poet William Ellery Channing, Hawthorne, and members of Emerson's household, especially his children.

IKEDA: In a late journal entry, Thoreau wrote, "You cannot buy a friend."[10] He was not, however, afraid to be alone. In an 1848 letter, he wrote, "Do not think that you have companions: know that you are alone in the world."[11]

True friendship is a bond between people capable of standing on their own two feet. Shakyamuni Buddha also says something beautiful on friendship. His disciple the venerable Ananda asks him, "Having good friends and practicing among them would be halfway to the mastery of the Buddha Way, would it not?" Surprisingly, Shakyamuni disagrees: "Having good friends does not constitute the midpoint to the Buddha Way. It constitutes all of the Buddha Way."[12] I believe Shakyamuni meant that the effort to make good friends goes hand in hand with improving oneself.

BOSCO: In Thoreau's journal, we find that nature took on all the qualities of a personal friend for him, and so there is no doubt that he, at least, would never have thought of himself as alone or lonely as long as he was alive out in nature.

As he reported in his journal on December 15, 1841, Thoreau believed his Concord world, which he considered as fair as the "Valhalla of the gods,"[13] was designed to answer his every question, satisfy his every yearning, and fulfill his every dream. On December 1, 1856, he confessed that he imaginatively embraced a "shrub oak with its scanty garment of leaves rising above the snow"[14] and fell in love with her, while, on April 23, 1857, he declared all nature to be his bride.[15]

IKEDA: In a journal entry on December 31, 1851, Thoreau wrote that the "earth I tread on is not a dead, inert mass. It is a body, has a spirit, is organic, and fluid to the influence of its spirit, and to whatever article of that spirit is in me."[16]

We must revive this sense of belonging to this great life entity, the Earth. Carson, who studied Thoreau's view of nature, said that no one attuned to the beauty and mystery of the Earth—scientist or not—can ever become jaded or lonely. This is why *Walden* will long be read as that rare textbook on the harmonious symbiosis of humanity and nature.

MYERSON: Thoreau's message has greater significance now than ever before.

COMMITTED TO ABOLITION

IKEDA: Thoreau turned his lucid eye not only to nature but to society. He was, for instance, a lifelong abolitionist. Thoreau played an active role in assisting runaway slaves to reach Canada.

MYERSON: Yes, he was a collaborator in the Underground Railroad system that crisscrossed the New England states in the 1850s and was one of the most outspoken and defiant members of his generation when the Fugitive Slave Law was enacted by Congress and implemented in Boston.

IKEDA: Thoreau defended John Brown when he was tried for treason, saying that Brown had the "courage to face his country herself when she was in the wrong."[17] In "Civil Disobedience," he wrote, "The only government that I recognize . . . is that power that establishes justice in the land, never that which establishes injustice."[18]

The Transcendentalists upheld the spiritual dignity of all human beings. Thoreau's sociopolitical philosophy demonstrates a flowering of their teachings.

Thought that strives for universality can lose its validity by becoming too abstract. In Thoreau's case, however, universal thought found expression in daily, social, and political contemplation and action.

MYERSON: In the late 1850s, Thoreau was as committed an abolitionist as any person alive in New England.

IKEDA: Aside from his involvement in abolition, Thoreau led a quiet life his remaining fifteen years after Walden. He improved the quality of the pencils produced by his family business until they were on par with the best from London. After his father's death, he helped the business prosper, thus contributing to the prosperity of the Concord pencil industry, which grew to thirteen firms.

He was a man of many talents. As Emerson said, "With his energy and practical ability he seemed born for great enterprise and for command."[19]

What are your thoughts on his work ethic?

MYERSON: To me, Thoreau's best thoughts on labor are contained in this passage in *Walden*'s first chapter: "The cost of a thing is the amount of what I will call life which is required to be exchanged for it, immediately or in the long run."[20] In other words, labor should be commensurate with what it costs, not in monetary terms but in terms of our lives and how we choose to spend them.

That is one reason why Thoreau turned to farming at Walden Pond to support himself: His labor not only provided his food, thus freeing him from hiring himself out for pay in order to buy things in town, but also literally rooted him to the Earth. He learned about nature while working, thus accomplishing two goals with one effort.

IKEDA: This, too, shows his pursuit of the true goal of life. From his mid-thirties, Thoreau's health weakened. Inhaling graphite in the pencil factory had harmed his lungs.

He died in his beloved Concord home on May 6, 1862, at forty-four. A friend who nursed him said he had never witnessed so joyful and peaceful a death.

Thoreau's last words are said to have been "moose" and "Indian." For a person like Thoreau, who had a great interest in American Indians, these seem fitting.

BOSCO: That is one of the subjects I find fascinating about Thoreau's later career: his attitude toward American Indians. In the nineteenth century, most native tribes had been displaced from the New England landscape. Occasionally finding arrowheads and other small indications of their former presence, Thoreau lamented the loss from New England of the great tribes with their knowledge of the Earth and of nature.

IKEDA: Their symbiosis with nature must have served him as a model.

BOSCO: Late in life, he began an extended series of notebooks on American Indians and in them copied, among other things, passages such as one I wish to share here. This particularly moving and poignant passage from March 23, 1856, not only suggests Thoreau's feelings on this subject but also draws attention to his views on the loss—through hunting, exploitation of resources, and excessive farming in the nineteenth century—of American Indian culture in New England. He considered it part and parcel of the diminishment of the natural world he traveled:

> I spend a considerable portion of my time observing the habits of
> the wild animals, my brute neighbors. By their various movements

and migrations they fetch the year about to me. Very significant are the flight of geese and the migration of suckers. . . . But when I consider that the nobler animals have been exterminated here,— the cougar, panther, lynx, wolverine, wolf, bear, moose, deer, the beaver, the turkey, etc., etc.,—I cannot but feel as if I lived in a tamed, and, as it were, emasculated country. Would not the motions of those larger and wilder animals have been more significant still? Is it not a maimed and imperfect nature that I am conversant with? As if I were to study a tribe of Indians that had lost all its warriors. Do not the forest and the meadow now lack expression, now that I never see nor think of the moose with a lesser forest on his head in the one, nor of the beaver in the other? When I think what were the various sounds and notes, the migrations and works, and changes of fur and plumage which ushered in the spring and marked the other seasons of the year, I am reminded that this my life in nature, this particular round of natural phenomena which I call a year, is lamentably incomplete. I listen to [a] concert in which so many parts are wanting.[21]

IKEDA: His regret over what was being lost filled this passage.

BOSCO: He went on to write:

The whole civilized country is to some extent turned into a city, and I am that citizen whom I pity. Many of those animal migrations and other phenomena by which the Indians marked the season are no longer to be observed. I seek acquaintance with Nature, to know her moods and manners. Primitive Nature is the most interesting to me. I take pains to know all the phenomena of the spring, for instance, thinking that I have here the entire poem, and then, to my chagrin, I hear that it is but an imperfect copy that I possess and have read, that my ancestors have torn out many of the first leaves and grandest passages, and mutilated it in many places. I should not like to think that some demigod had come before me and picked out some of the best of the stars.

I wish to know an entire heaven and an entire earth. All the great trees and beasts, fishes and fowl are gone. The streams, perchance, are somewhat shrunk.[22]

IKEDA: Unfortunately, confirming Thoreau's concern for the future, the twentieth century became a century of destruction. We must make the twenty-first century one of respect for the dignity of life.

To achieve this, we must ask what we really need and what we must reform. Thoreau's life offers us a new model for living and is certain to shine with increased radiance in the years to come.

Reading and Human Development

A Reputation Blossoms

BOSCO: The inaugural Ikeda Forum for Intercultural Dialogue was held at the Boston Research Center for the 21st Century (renamed the Ikeda Center for Peace, Learning, and Dialogue in 2009) on October 1 and 2, 2004.

IKEDA: I am grateful to both of you and the Thoreau Society for cooperating with this undertaking. As founder of the Boston Research Center, I am delighted that we have created a new dialogue venue to bring together intellectuals from many areas of American life in establishing spiritual bonds between East and West.

BOSCO: And we are grateful for the message you sent to the forum, the goal of which is to ensure the future life of the vision and spirit of world peace that you have demonstrated in your numerous intercultural dialogues.

This first forum was a great success thanks to the participation of a large number of scholars in the field of Thoreau-Emerson studies. Dialogues on important topics like the profound philosophical elements that the thought of Thoreau and Emerson shares with Nichiren Buddhism were significant. I am certain that this is only the first step in deep, forward-looking, East-West philosophical exchanges.

IKEDA: As the forum symbolized, Thoreau's thought had a worldwide influence and history-altering impact in many fields. It is still enlightening people today. Ironically, his work and thought gained little attention during his lifetime.

MYERSON: The attention paid to Thoreau shortly after his death was unimpressive. Such public responses as Emerson's essay on him in the *Atlantic Monthly* and James Russell Lowell's reviews of his works portrayed him to the general public as a somewhat priggish and humorless loner. He was not the "heroic" type of American.

IKEDA: But later, Thoreau's reputation spread throughout the world. Like a seed planted deep in the ground that germinates, takes root, and grows into a great tree benefiting many, Thoreau's thought brings blessings to humanity to this day.

BOSCO: A splendid poetic image that vividly expresses the way the estimation of a man who during his life in Concord was virtually invisible blossomed after his death.

IKEDA: Thoreau's thought evolved through long years of nature study, reading, and reflection. But he seems to have worried about what meaning his spiritual life had for society.

BOSCO: In true Socratic fashion, Thoreau was ever challenging himself to identify meaning in his life, in his relationships, and in the mark he believed he had a responsibility to make on history. For him, the unexamined life was not worth living and was not an option to be entertained by him or by anyone else.

An Expanding Sphere of Influence

IKEDA: Again, he was ahead of his time.

BOSCO: Thoreau chided himself in his journal on November 16, 1850, for being too little involved in the activities of the bustling life around him and for being unclear about the mark he should make on the world:

> I have no more distinctness or pointedness in my yearnings than an expanding bud, which does indeed point to flower and fruit, to summer and autumn, but is aware of the warm sun and spring influence only. I feel ripe for something, yet do nothing, can't discover what that thing is. I feel fertile merely. It is seedtime with me. I have lain fallow long enough.[1]

IKEDA: This passage gives us a good idea of Thoreau's exasperation over how his talents remained unfulfilled and unrecognized by society. But great people and philosophies not in step with their times later come to shine on the stage of history. It is frequently the case that their very perspicacity and excellence hinder their being easily understood.

BOSCO: In spite of Thoreau's concerns that he felt "fertile merely" and that he had "lain fallow long enough," there can be no question that he indeed exerted a profound influence on those generations of Americans that followed his own. His sphere of influence was somewhat limited in his time primarily to a circle of local friends and neighbors: Emerson and his family, including his wife Lidian, aunt Mary Moody Emerson, and children, especially Edward Waldo; Bronson Alcott, Hawthorne, and Channing; and those numerous, now-obscure persons to whom he refers throughout his journal with whom he talked regularly and with whom he spent many days and evenings walking through Concord's meadows and woods, and along her river banks.

MYERSON: Over the near century and a half since his death, Thoreau has emerged as a figure of great importance on the stage of history. A wide range of individuals from all walks of life has appropriated his ideas and ideals.

THE THOREAU REVIVAL BEGINS

IKEDA: Thoreau delivered more than seventy lectures in Concord and other parts of Massachusetts, but they failed to enhance his reputation as lecturing did Emerson's. Thoreau wrote extensively, including magazine essays and his personal journal of two million words.

Yet just two of his works were published during his lifetime. Only in the twentieth century did *Walden* come to be regarded as one of the masterpieces of American literature.

Some of his other works did capture some attention before that. How did that come about?

MYERSON: After the Civil War, Thoreau's reputation lay in the hands of a few men who did their best to get his works into print. Both *A Week on the Concord and Merrimack Rivers* and *Walden* were reissued in 1862, and other books—some of which Thoreau had been preparing on his deathbed to ensure an income for his family—soon followed: *Excursions* (1863), *The Maine Woods* (1864), *Cape Cod* (1865), *Letters to Various Persons* (1865), and *A Yankee in Canada with Anti-Slavery and Reform Papers* (1866). While these books sold moderately well, it was not until Harrison Gray Otis Blake read through Thoreau's journal that the real Thoreau revival began.

Blake was a minister-educator on close terms with Thoreau. As is well known, they corresponded for years.

Thoreau's younger sister, Sophia, took good care of the journal manuscript after Thoreau's death. When she herself was about to die, she gave it to Blake, who subsequently published it.

Blake chose selections from the journal and arranged them

under seasonal headings in four books: *Early Spring in Massachusetts* (1881), *Summer* (1884), *Winter* (1888), and *Autumn* (1892). These books established Thoreau as a naturalist, thus beginning the process of giving him a place in the pantheon of New England authors. Collected editions of his writings appeared in 1894 and 1906, when the complete journal was published in fourteen volumes from Houghton Mifflin, the publisher of all the major New England authors, including Emerson.

A Shared Love of Books

IKEDA: After Thoreau's death, these publications spread his fame throughout the world. The most brilliant spoken words fade away, but great thoughts—and the spirit they contain—can last forever in print. The desire to pass on wisdom and valuable ideas to posterity has moved me to engage in dialogues with people from throughout the world and publish these dialogues.

Let's turn our attention to the attitudes of Emerson and Thoreau toward books, exploring their reading habits.

MYERSON: Emerson and Thoreau considered books to be important, both for intellectual and spiritual reasons. Both men were involved in local reading clubs, and Emerson served for many years on the Concord town library committee. Indeed, when Emerson was chosen to give the opening address at the dedication of the Concord Free Public Library in 1873, eleven years after Thoreau's death, he noted that his friend had been an "excellent reader" and that "no man would have rejoiced more than he in the event of this day."[2]

In Thoreau's words, "Books are the treasured wealth of the world and the fit inheritance of generations and nations."[3]

IKEDA: Thoreau's love of reading, as evidenced by the numbers of books he borrowed from the library during his time at Harvard, is well known. He also absorbed a great deal of knowledge from

Emerson's huge library, the extracts and notes he made from his reading running to five- or six-thousand pages.

One chapter of *Walden*, which discusses reading, contains the following:

> No wonder that Alexander carried the *Iliad* with him on his expeditions in a precious casket. A written word is the choicest of relics.[4]

MYERSON: Two studies of Thoreau's bibliophilia make this point clear: In a 1983 listing of the books Thoreau is known to have owned, Walter Harding gives 397 titles; and in a 1988 catalogue of books Thoreau is known to have consulted or read, Robert Sattelmeyer identifies 1,478 titles.

We can also see how important books were to Thoreau by examining how they affected his relationship with his alma mater, Harvard College. A letter to the Harvard librarian, Jared Sparks, in 1849 speaks eloquently about Thoreau's debt to books:

> I wish to get permission to take books from the College library to Concord where I reside. I am encouraged to ask this . . . *because I have chosen letters for my profession.* . . . Moreover, though books are to some extent my stock and tools, I have not the usual means with which to purchase them. . . . I ask only that the University may help to finish the education, whose foundation she has helped to lay.[5]

When in 1859 his classmates appealed for donations to the college library, Thoreau responded with a gift of five dollars, writing that, "I would gladly give more, but this exceeds my income from all sources together for the last four months."[6] Books mattered to him.

IKEDA: Five dollars was a big sum for Thoreau at the time. But realizing the importance of a library, he did the best he could. I understand exactly how he felt.

MYERSON: What are your memories, President Ikeda, related to books?

IKEDA: As a young man, I scrimped and saved from my small salary to collect books in which I had a special interest. As time went by, my collection grew quite large.

I have donated my library to the two universities I founded, Soka University of Japan and Soka University of America. The library is the heart and soul of a university. I will be happy if my gift serves even slightly as scholarly and spiritual nourishment for the students.

Where did Thoreau's love of books come from?

BOSCO: I believe that Thoreau developed his interest in reading partly from the conditions of a time in which reading, like home schooling, was a primary form of education, partly out of personal intellectual curiosity that is impressive even to this day, and partly from the influence of Emerson, who emphasized the importance of reading to him and others of his generation.

In his lecture "Some Good Books," Emerson stated:

> In books, I have the history or the energy of the past. Angels they are to us of entertainment, sympathy, and provocation. With them, many of us spend the most of our life: these silent and wise, these tractable prophets, historians, and singers, whose embalmed life is the highest feat of art, who now cast their moonlight illumination over solitude, weariness, and fallen fortunes.[7]

Reading supplied Thoreau with the history and "energy of the past," and he could appreciate books and the good literature preserved in them as, to paraphrase Emerson, angelic influences. All forms of good reading provided Thoreau with complements to the evolution of his ideas as well as with the means to probe deeply into himself and better understand his relationship with nature.

IKEDA: When I was young, my mentor urged me to make reading and reflection a habit. He constantly insisted on the importance of books.

Right up to his death, he would ask me what I had read that day and what I thought of it. This discipline has become a precious treasure for me.

The books I read in my youth offered me great nourishment. They refined my intellect, tempered my spirit, and inspired me to develop myself.

MYERSON: Thoreau recognized the ways in which books provoke us into thinking. He said:

> To read well, that is, to read true books in a true spirit, is a noble exercise, and one that will task the reader more than any exercise which the customs of the day esteem.[8]

Or, as Thoreau reformulated his advice, "Books must be read as deliberately and reservedly as they were written."[9]

IKEDA: My mentor used to say that you are not really reading unless you capture the author's personality, philosophy, and views of humanity, the world, and the cosmos. Unless you understand the author's circumstances, you will perhaps be misled.

He taught me how to read the deeper meaning an author is trying to convey. Reading should be an earnest dialogue between reader and author, a spiritual undertaking that ultimately reveals the reader's inner world. As Thoreau insisted, it is important to choose good books and read them earnestly.

He also described the classics as "golden words, which the wisest men of antiquity have uttered, and whose worth the wise of every succeeding age have assured us of."[10]

Handed down through the ages, great books embody the light of profound wisdom and spirit. In addition to the classics and sacred texts, Thoreau eagerly absorbed all the latest knowledge of the America of his time.

BOSCO: Thoreau relished the lessons he took from the classics, but he also read widely in the works of modern poets, essayists, and scientists, and was an avid reader of the sacred texts of both Eastern and Western cultures. He knew the Gospels, Shakespeare, Montaigne, and the major writers of his time, as well as sayings attributed to Shakyamuni Buddha and Zoroaster, the wisdom of Confucius, and the dramatic verses of many Hindu texts.

IKEDA: I am fascinated by the extent of knowledge Emerson and Thoreau accumulated on Eastern philosophy and thought, and their eagerness to adopt it and introduce it to their contemporary Americans. The Eastern classics and sacred texts with which Thoreau was familiar were numerous.

BOSCO: He owned and read, for example, an edition of *Le Bhâgavata Purâna* translated into French by Eugène Burnouf in 1853 and an edition of the *Institutes of Hindu Law; Or the Ordinances of Menu* translated into English by Sir William Jones and published in London in 1825, both of which Thoreau bequeathed to Emerson, along with several other Eastern texts.

It is fair to say that Thoreau learned much from reading these texts. Throughout his journal, he reveals his intellectual and spiritual debt to their influence by quoting from them regularly; in fact, in reading these quotations, one is often left with the impression that these texts supplied Thoreau with some of his most enduring insights into human nature, for we hear their echoes throughout his writings. An illustration of such influence is the following quotation, which succinctly expresses one of Thoreau's major themes in *Walden*, and which Thoreau identified in a May 6, 1851, journal entry as taken from a commentary on the Hindu text *Sankhya Karika*: "By external knowledge worldly distinction is acquired; by internal knowledge, liberation."[11]

MYERSON: There is one area related to this in which Emerson and Thoreau were in disagreement.

IKEDA: What would that be?

MYERSON: Translations. Thoreau argued:

> Those who have not learned to read the ancient classics in the language in which they were written must have a very imperfect knowledge of the history of the human race.[12]

IKEDA: Himself a polyglot, with knowledge of classical Greek and Latin, French, Italian, Spanish, and German, Thoreau felt it important to read things in the original. He said that because the classical languages were enlightening, it was useful even for farmers and ordinary people to commit to memory and be able to use a word or two of Latin as conversation permitted.[13]

MYERSON: But for Emerson, who championed American literary nationalism, "What is really best in any book is translatable,— any real insight or broad human sentiment." He desired the "great metropolitan English speech" and concluded:

> I should as soon think of swimming across Charles River when I wish to go to Boston, as of reading all my books in originals when I have them rendered for me in my mother tongue.[14]

THE LOST ART OF READING?

IKEDA: In my youth, when Japanese militarism prevailed, learning foreign languages was strictly forbidden. That is why Japanese of my generation tend to sympathize with Emerson's view. Nonetheless, I realize that certain nuances are incomprehensible unless we can read works in the original.

Thoreau eventually became familiar with literature from many places and times, but Emerson's works must have exerted the greatest influence on him as a young man.

BOSCO: One of the most influential volumes that Thoreau read while in college was Emerson's *Nature*, which he studied immediately after its publication in 1836. Emerson's advice remained with him and influenced his thoughts long after his first reading of *Nature*.

IKEDA: Those are lucky who, in their youth, discover outstanding, life-altering books. Such books establish lifelong guidelines, become prized treasures, and nourish one's life.

This is why the tendency among today's youth to shun reading is especially disturbing. In Japan, as elsewhere, the growing distance between young people and reading is a serious problem.

BOSCO: In an age such as ours, when knowledge seems to be instantaneously—if indiscriminately—transmitted in news bites and the banter of so-called talking heads on television or via the Internet and across e-mail networks, it is interesting to think about how Thoreau's reputation has been preserved and promoted through the generations by readers. Today, many people seem to have lost the art of reading, or, perhaps, they were never introduced to the new and wonderful worlds that reading good literature can open for anyone.

IKEDA: We adults hold responsibility for young people's aversion to reading. Children who have even once experienced the unknown world of adventure that reading offers sooner or later turn to books on their own initiative. This is why, through my speeches and other means, I constantly try to introduce youth to superior works of world literature from all periods and to the great ideas they contain.

Victor Hugo said that depriving people of the freedom of the press is tantamount to depriving them of food. Without the power and freedom of the press, there can be no happiness. The end result, he said, is "misdirection, shipwreck, and disaster."[15]

Hugo proclaimed the necessity of what we now call the freedom of publication, expression, thought, and debate. As he said, the decay of this freedom leads to the debility of civilization and the loss of spiritual and intellectual health in society.

Because of their shared reading, Emerson and Thoreau could discuss the wise and great of past and present, thus turning their search for the truth into a new philosophy.

Walden and "Civil Disobedience"

A POET OF NATURE

IKEDA: *Walden* has enchanted people the world over with its lively, sometimes humorous descriptions of Thoreau's self-sufficient life in the woods. The book reveals how Thoreau's refined soul appreciated the wonder of nature and heartbeat of all things.

His was the radiant world of a mind open to nature and the universe. I am especially attracted to his poetic descriptions of spring and morning, written as if the energy of life itself flowed through his pen:

> The first sparrow of spring! The year beginning with younger hope than ever! The faint silvery warblings heard over the partially bare and moist fields from the blue-bird, the song-sparrow, and the red-wing, as if the last flakes of winter tinkled as they fell! . . . The brooks sing carols and glees to the spring. The marsh-hawk, sailing low over the meadow, is already seeking the first slimy life that awakes. The sinking sound of melting snow is heard in all dells, and the ice dissolves apace in the ponds.[1]

Throughout *Walden*, we hear nature's symphonic poem in the form of forest and pond and their inhabitants. His skill as a master poet enlivens the entire book.

BOSCO: For some—and I include myself in this category—Thoreau is the supreme poet-naturalist, the lover of nature who identifies completely with all aspects of nature's wondrous panorama. His prose writings, especially his journal, constitute one extended hymn of praise directed toward nature and her ability to liberate the individual from all confining aspects of culture.

As a journal entry from May 10, 1853, indicates, he literally prayed for the continuance of his ability to find himself described and thus identified through nature's tropes and symbols:

> If I am overflowing with life, am rich in experience for which I lack expression, then nature will be my language full of poetry,—all nature will *fable*, and every natural phenomenon be a myth. . . . I pray for such inward experience as will make nature significant.[2]

IKEDA: Thoreau's reactions to animals and insects reveal the joy he felt in living as part of nature. He considered the field mice that visited his place real friends and allowed them to scamper over his boots and crawl on his clothes.

With great humor, he described the hornets that wintered in his cabin. Most of us would be horrified at the sight of a single hornet, but Thoreau wrote, "I even felt complimented by their regarding my house as a desirable shelter."[3] I think he was sympathetic to insects and all creatures because he perceived the irreplaceable light of life deep within them all.

MYERSON: *Walden* is full of Thoreau's love of nature and living things. Your attempts, President Ikeda, to encourage others to appreciate the natural world and its harmony through your photographs are similar to Thoreau's attempts to achieve the same purpose through the words that comprise *Walden*. Both you and

Thoreau use your abilities to present the natural world in such a way as to show humankind's harmony with it.

IKEDA: But my photographs are just the work of an amateur taking pictures when he has a spare moment or from the window of a moving vehicle. Although I do not have much time to pursue photography, I strive to preserve the spirit of poetry in these "dialogues with nature." I look through my viewfinder hoping to eternalize the brilliance of each instant in the natural world.

MYERSON: Thoreau's love of nature came from his study of its harmony with humankind—of his realization that the natural world contains lessons by which we can live our daily lives. This belief in the connection between us and the natural world, and the importance of our realizing our roles as stewards and protectors of the natural world, is a major reason why Thoreau and his writings have been so influential on the ecological writers and activists of the present day.

IKEDA: Buddhism, too, teaches the oneness of humankind and nature, insisting that a symbiotic relationship must exist between them.

THE NATURAL WORLD AS TEACHER

IKEDA: Thoreau's way of life at Walden Pond was simplicity itself. He kept his furniture to a minimum and chose clothes that would last, no matter how old they were.

At first, he ate bakery bread but later baked his own. He cultivated his own beans and potatoes.

His lifestyle would be hard on most people today. He harmonized his daily rhythm with that of the natural world, rising early and, after bathing in the pond, working in his garden. After reading, he bathed again in the afternoon and took a walk in whatever direction he desired. At night, he fell asleep to the rustling of forest leaves and the soft scuffling of animals.

Because Thoreau set a course for his soul through penetrating self-examination and oneness with nature, *Walden* reminds many people today about important things they have lost.

What was the site of his cabin like?

MYERSON: The site is near the north shore of the pond on a low, thickly wooded hill. It is about a mile-and-a-half south of Concord, close enough that he could easily visit the town but far enough away that he could ignore its existence. Thoreau chose to move to Walden Pond because Emerson made the land available to him.

IKEDA: Also in a forest, Shakyamuni Buddha long ago pondered the meaning of human life. By the way, it is said that Indian civilization was born in the forest. The Indian tradition of refining one's wisdom in a forest setting was the origin of abandoning secular living for religious contemplation.

Not just forests but the whole natural world can be a great teacher for us. In his *Geography of Human Life*, written in 1903, Makiguchi urged us to learn how to live by studying the relationship between humanity and nature.

Reading *Walden* always makes me yearn for the place. Does it still look much as it did?

MYERSON: Thanks to the heroic efforts of the Massachusetts Department of Environmental Management and the Walden Pond State Reservation, the land around the pond has been restored to something like its nineteenth-century state. Also, through the efforts of the Walden Woods Project, lands connected to Walden Woods are being placed under permanent nature conservancy restrictions forbidding all development.

I, too, have worked to preserve the environment Thoreau lived in and am happy to say that several projects undertaken during my presidency of the Thoreau Society (1992–96) to preserve the Concord area have been successful.

BOSCO: Because I am currently president of the Thoreau Society (2000–04) and chairman of the Friends of Walden Pond Committee (2001–04), I find myself passing or visiting and walking around Walden Pond on a regular, sometimes weekly, basis. To this day, I continue to be struck by the smallness of the pond.

This impression has been with me since I first visited it in the 1960s. Its small size contrasts sharply with the genuine largeness of the lessons Thoreau imparts to me every time I read *Walden*.

IKEDA: Many others share your impression.

Choosing His Own Way

BOSCO: With Thoreau, there is no inconsistency between theory and practice. He believed his stay at Walden Pond was an act of deliberate living and fulfilled his desire to, as he phrased it, "front only the essential facts of life."[4]

At Walden, Thoreau's life was sublime. He plumbed the depths of human nature. Succeeding against all odds and the expectations of his friends and neighbors, he exercised his right to choose a way of life for himself.

IKEDA: Thoreau's writings remind me of Montaigne's *Essays*, which are observations on humanity and social action based on the author's extensive reading of ancient and contemporary works and on serious self-reflection. I see the quintessential element in Thoreau's essays as likewise a challenging, thorough pursuit of truth based on his experience.

This also reminds me of Makiguchi's insistence that one must verify one's beliefs in the context of daily life. He took the lead in putting this principle into practice himself.

BOSCO: That idea resonates with Thoreau's philosophy. He was conscious of separating himself from those philosophers who theorized life but did not live it and separating his philosophy from those schools or systems that advocated certain ideas or ideals but never tested their efficacy or their limits in the real world.

I have already commented on his excellent qualities as a poet. For many of his readers and followers, Thoreau in *Walden* is the master prophet of self-culture—the fashioner of a unique form of American identity. Of course, people who would like to live their own lives as he did need not take up residence at Walden.

One of the lessons that I have taken from *Walden*—and that I try hard to impress upon my students—is that the story of Thoreau's stay there is *his* story, not one that we should try to repeat literally. Thus, for those alive today, Thoreau's story is one that shows us how important it is for each of us to seek and find our own Walden Pond.

IKEDA: In *Walden*, Thoreau spoke of a young acquaintance who "thought he should live as I did." Discouraging the notion, Thoreau said:

> I would not have any one adopt my mode of living on any account; for, beside that before he has fairly learned it I may have found out another for myself, I desire that there may be as many different persons in the world as possible; but I would have each one be very careful to find out and pursue his own way, and not his father's or his mother's or his neighbor's instead.[5]

In this vigorous proclamation of independence, Thoreau advised all of us not to copy others but to gain a firm hold on one's own way of life.

UNIVERSAL APPLICATIONS

MYERSON: Thoreau's attention to global citizenship, too, is another trait worthy of special notice. Although Thoreau remained in Concord for most of his life, he was insistent that his observations of local phenomena had universal applications; or, as he wrote in

"The Pond in Winter," the "pure Walden water is mingled with the sacred water of the Ganges."[6] This is one example of his universal approach.

Like Emerson and many of the Transcendentalists, Thoreau searched for connections among various cultures. Just as Emerson had been pushed in this direction by the Biblical criticism of Germany, which practiced a type of comparative religion, Thoreau was made a comparatist by his wide reading and by his discernment of similarities among the stories told in each culture.

In other words, the fact that different cultures and religions shared similar stories or traits suggested a common ancestral story behind all of them. This reinforced Thoreau's belief, already held by the Transcendentalists, that God was present in all things.

IKEDA: His open-mindedness put him ahead of his time. Society was unready to accept his revolutionary ideas, which today seem quite natural to many.

My mentor likewise advocated global citizenship when the Cold War was growing increasingly serious. Though he never had the opportunity to travel outside Japan, he always kept his resolution to eliminate suffering from the entire world. Determined that no one remain trapped in unhappiness, that no one be sacrificed, he urged everyone to become global citizens and transcend national and ethnic interests.

This advocacy was rooted in his resolute resistance to authority and consistent speaking out for justice. Because of this, the militarist government unjustly imprisoned him.

BOSCO: Thoreau explained his ideas on the topic in the following famous passage from "Civil Disobedience":

> There will never be a really free and enlightened State, until the State comes to recognize the individual as a higher and independent power, from which all its own power and authority are derived, and treats him accordingly.[7]

Here, Thoreau was surely commenting on the limitations of the State, but he was also, and more particularly, remarking on the importance of the individual's recognition of the "higher and independent power" that we each possess. Unless the individual realizes his or her own power, acknowledges that such power comes only from within, and *then* transforms the world through the appropriate exercise of that power, the State becomes dominant and creates a society characterized by oppression and the crassest variety of materialism.

It is in this context that Thoreau's simple refusal to pay his poll tax rises to the level of a powerful, heroic action that has inspired men of conscience ever since. It is in this context, too, that Thoreau demonstrates for us the practical application of his theory on important issues that affect our everyday lives.

THE "TRUE PLACE FOR A JUST MAN"

IKEDA: It was, I believe, when Thoreau was living at Walden that he was thrown in jail for refusing to pay the poll tax. He stated, "I did not pay a tax to or recognize the authority of the state which buys and sells men, women, and children, like cattle at the door of its senate-house."[8]

MYERSON: It was in July 1846, just one year after he started to live in his hut on Walden Pond. After he gave up living in the woods, he lectured on his jail time. The content of the lectures was later published in a magazine as "Civil Disobedience."

IKEDA: I think the following three principles summarize Thoreau's message in "Civil Disobedience":

- No government has the right to threaten human dignity.
- We must resolutely struggle against oppressive authority of all kinds.
- The power of an individual can change the world.

Thoreau embodied these truths. Expressing the first, he said in "Civil Disobedience" that we are human beings first, subjects of civil authority second.

In feudal thirteen-century Japan, Nichiren, facing a storm of oppression, proclaimed, "Even if it seems that, because I was born in the ruler's domain, I follow him in my actions, I will never follow him in my heart."[9] This passage is included in *The Birthright of Man*, compiled by UNESCO to commemorate the twentieth anniversary, in 1968, of the Universal Declaration of Human Rights.

BOSCO: It demonstrates a noble spirit.

Reflecting on his vocation as a writer, Thoreau entered the following statement in his journal on August 19, 1851: "How vain it is to sit down to write when you have not stood up to live!"[10] To carry out our own work sincerely, we should all bear this in mind.

I want to return to his journal entry for January 5, 1856: "Nature is full of genius, full of the divinity."[11] The importance of this statement for me is that in it Thoreau expressed the guiding principle of his life, which variously served him as a personal version of the Ten Commandments and as a gauge of the quality of his actions.

Thoreau believed that his actions always had to be consistent with the goodness and harmony he perceived in nature. In this respect, he was not only a philosopher but also, I believe, a profoundly religious thinker.

IKEDA: Being true to his beliefs came first for Thoreau. Instead of frightening him, imprisonment only ignited his fiery will to fight. He stated in a famous line from "Civil Disobedience," "Under a government which imprisons any unjustly, the true place for a just man is also a prison."[12]

With the spiritual power of speech, Nichiren told the State authorities straight to their faces that people in governmental and religious capacities should be working in the interest of the ordinary masses.

Makiguchi and Toda remained unbroken by the obstinate oppression of the militarist authorities precisely because they were heirs to Nichiren's spirit. In 1957, the year before Toda's death, I, too, was mercilessly subjected, on trumped-up charges, to the experience of imprisonment.

WHO CAN CHANGE THE WORLD?

MYERSON: These experiences supplied the spiritual source for the SGI peace and human rights movements. The main theme of your novel *The Human Revolution* is that a "great human revolution in just a single individual will help achieve a change in the destiny of a nation and further, will enable a change in the destiny of all humankind."[13] Thoreau, as he stated the case in "Civil Disobedience," wrote that the U.S. government does not have the "vitality and force of a single living man; for a single man can bend it to his will."[14]

Both Emerson and Thoreau firmly believed, as you do, that before we can have change in society we must have change in people; that is, rather than waiting for legislators to provide us with just and fair laws, which will force humankind to act better, we must ourselves—as individuals—become better people, for then we will make better laws.

BOSCO: No matter how one chooses to use Thoreau's works and the world in which he lived as means to define the essential character of the man, there can be no doubt that Thoreau finally appeals to each and every one of us as an ideal extension of ourselves. Although he died in 1862, he still speaks directly to us.

The hold Thoreau has exerted over the popular imagination for the past century and a half is to my mind partly the result of the way he tried to discover truths through his own way of living and partly the result of the way his message—to test life in all its baseness and in all its sublimity—provides a liberating influence on the lives of those who still may suffer from resignation and perhaps even "quiet desperation."[15] Thoreau stands as one of America's great voices championing the principled life.

IKEDA: In "Civil Disobedience," Thoreau wrote, "O for a man who is a *man*, and, as my neighbor says, has a bone in his back which you cannot pass your hand through!"[16] People today must stop and look at how they are living, then redirect themselves toward their development as human beings who are truly *human beings*. Thoreau's works indeed provide the key to this necessary transformation and the inner force that effects it.

CONVERSATION EIGHT

Beyond the Pulpit

STARTING OUT WITH EMERSON

IKEDA: Emerson, like Thoreau and Whitman, was one of my favorite authors as a young man. I read a collection of his essays right after the war, when I was eighteen or nineteen.

My mentor urged me to read him carefully. I still have some of Emerson's works in my study, right where I can easily reach them, and have taken numerous opportunities to quote him in my speeches to young people.

BOSCO: My first serious acquaintance with Emerson's writings occurred in a course on the history of American life and letters that I took when I was a junior in college. I was actually a philosophy—not a literature—major in college, and earned my master's degree in philosophy in the areas of ethics and aesthetics.

Emerson's writings and ideas struck me in a way that nothing I had read before ever had. After taking my doctorate in English in 1975, I became an editor of the Emerson Papers at the Houghton

Library of Harvard University. That was in 1977, and I have been reading Emerson, editing his unpublished manuscripts, and including him in every American literature and intellectual history course that I have taught ever since.

IKEDA: Both of you have been president of the Ralph Waldo Emerson Society and have written and published extensively on him.

BOSCO: For the greater part of my career, Emerson has been my major figure. My professional interest in Thoreau came late in my career.

MYERSON: I, too, entered Thoreau's world through my interest in Emerson.

IKEDA: The American philosopher and educator John Dewey considered Emerson a philosopher of democracy. Much of Emerson's thought, especially ideas like self-reliance, continue to exert worldwide influence.

INDIVIDUAL REFORM MUST COME FIRST

MYERSON: Over the past decade, Dr. Bosco and I have worked together on a number of important academic projects relating to Emerson. (These include *The Later Lectures of Ralph Waldo Emerson, 1843–71*, published in 2001, and *The Emerson Brothers: A Fraternal Biography in Letters*, published in 2006.) In 2003, we were joint chairmen of the celebrations of the bicentennial of Emerson's birth.

Emerson blazed the path to the American Renaissance, which I think can be called the first time in American letters and history when writers sincerely challenged the values of the world around them. At the time, there were two approaches to reform. Some advocated passing good and noble laws that, if abided by, would make the people better. Others argued that improving the people was the way to pass good and noble laws.

Many reformers believed that legislating social justice would change human society and views of legislation. Emerson and Thoreau, however, passionately argued that social reform becomes possible only after the reform of the individual.

IKEDA: In 1840, a group of Transcendentalists, including Bronson Alcott and George Ripley, gathered at the Emerson home to plan the utopian cooperative called the Brook Farm Institute of Agriculture and Education. Emerson refused participation to the end.

In a journal entry for October 17, 1840, he wrote: "I do not wish to remove from my present prison to a prison a little larger. I wish to break all prisons."[1]

He was warning that without reform of the human being, even the best-ordered society will breed only new forms of imprisonment. The history of the twentieth century, reinforcing Emerson's cry, revealed how excessive pursuit of radical reform—for example, the socialist revolution—will bring about enormous sacrifice and suffering.

A TIGHT-KNIT FAMILY

IKEDA: You mentioned the correspondence of the Emerson brothers. Deep brotherly affection supported Emerson throughout the hardships of his youth.

MYERSON: Yes. Emerson was born in Boston on May 25, 1803, the second son of William, a minister, and his wife, Ruth. His father, a liberal Concord-born minister active in the city's intellectual and social life, died on May 12, 1811, putting the family in financial straits. Ralph was just seven at the time.

Mrs. Emerson was forced to take in boarders to help make ends meet. In 1817, Emerson entered Harvard College with financial assistance from the school, which required that he serve as the college president's freshman aide. He also earned money by teaching in schools for young people during breaks from classes.

IKEDA: He was impatient with classmates who lauded student life. Unlike them, he never had enough time to study.

This reminds me of how the young Makiguchi traveled to Otaru, on the island of Hokkaido, Japan, to attend the Hokkaido Normal School. He supported himself by working as an orderly in the local police station, where he was known as the Studious Errand Boy. Proud of this nickname, he studied hard and never wasted time.

During the war, as my older brothers were called away, I, at fourteen, had to help the family by going to work. After the war, I kept working and attended night classes. Those experiences made me feel closer to Emerson.

BOSCO: As you know, for the past several years, Dr. Myerson and I have been editing the unpublished correspondence of Emerson and his three brothers: William, Edward, and Charles (published as *The Emerson Brothers: A Fraternal Biography in Letters*, 2006).

What we have learned so far from this large body of correspondence is interesting biographically. The brothers, it appears, were genuinely close, with each successively providing financial or other forms of assistance to the next in line for preparatory school and college. Their letters reveal immense respect for one another and for their mother.

IKEDA: The brothers were blessed with a mother who, while struggling financially, managed to put three of them, Ralph, William, and Edward, through Harvard. A letter she wrote William as he was about to enter college expresses both a mother's care and the wish that he would study hard and grow into a fine person:

My Dear Son,—You did right to give me so early a proof of your affection as to write me the first week of your College life. Everything respecting you is doubtless interesting to me, but your domestic arrangements the least of anything, as these make no part of the man or the character any further than he learns humility from his dependence on such trifles as *Convenient accommodations* for his happiness. You, I trust, will rise superior to these little things, for though small indeed, they consume much time that might be appropriated to better purpose and far nobler pursuits.[2]

Her letter expresses a mother's deep love, philosophy, and prayers, and suggests that behind every great person is a great mother.

An Uneasy Fit With the Ministry

BOSCO: Although William, Edward, and Charles eventually pursued law careers, they all seem to have grown up expecting that at least one of the four brothers would carry on the ministerial tradition that had characterized the Emerson line for several generations. The boys' father, paternal grandfather, and great-grandfathers had previously occupied important pulpits in Boston, Malden, and Concord.

William, as the eldest brother, made an initial effort to become a minister, primarily by going abroad to study theology and philosophy in Germany. When it became clear to the family that he was not going to pursue a career in the ministry after all, the clerical mantle fell to Waldo, as he was known in the family, who prepared for the ministry and eventually served as pastor of Boston's prestigious Second Church until he resigned that post in 1832.

IKEDA: For a time, he taught at a girls school. Then, at twenty-one, deciding to become a minister, he entered Harvard Divinity School.

He gave up the ministry, however, at twenty-nine. This was one of his turning points. What motivated his resignation?

MYERSON: In 1825–26, he studied theology and divinity at Harvard and, on October, 10, 1826, was licensed to preach. Emerson occupied various pulpits over the next two years.

He also met and fell in love with Ellen Louisa Tucker of Concord, New Hampshire. Both strands of his life came together in 1829: He was ordained junior pastor of the prestigious Second Church on March 11, and he married Ellen on September 30.

Though happy, the marriage was marred by Ellen's worsening tuberculosis. She died on February 8, 1831.

Emerson returned to his ministerial duties with a heavy heart. He disliked all the social responsibilities of his position, particularly the regular visitations to parishioners, and he disagreed with his parish over the administration of the Lord's Supper, which he felt had become too ritualized.

BOSCO: He was pleased to be "called" to serve at the Second Church, for it was a prestigious appointment that provided him and his young wife with financial security and social respect. But Emerson was never fully satisfied with preaching traditional Christianity, even when it took the form of liberal Unitarianism.

As a matter of conscience, as well as an early indication of the Transcendental idealism that he would champion later in his career, he felt that traditional Christianity denied what he would later define as the "infinitude of the private man."[3]

MYERSON: Additionally, Emerson thought that, as it had become institutionalized in its various denominations, traditional Christianity made individuals more and more dependent on the past as opposed to becoming active agents in creating a new future for the human race.

IKEDA: The life of religion depends on whether it serves humanity, whether it provides strong support for human beings suffering amid the contradictions of life. In his journal, Emerson voiced the pain of having to go against his beliefs to join the formalities and rituals of the church. He wrote on January 10, 1831: "It is the best part of the man, I sometimes think, that revolts most against his being a minister. His good revolts from official goodness."[4]

RELIGION BY AND FOR THE PEOPLE

MYERSON: In September 1832, Emerson took a decisive step in a sermon on the Lord's Supper:

> Freedom is the essence of Christianity. It has for its object simply to make men good and wise. Its institutions should be as flexible as the wants of men. That form out of which the life and suitableness have departed should be as worthless in its eyes as the dead leaves that are falling around us.[5]

IKEDA: I deeply sympathize with this cry from the depths of Emerson's soul. The SGI has opposed a Buddhist clergy that, invoking tradition and authority, attempted to control practitioners. We are convinced that, instead of people existing for the sake of religion, religion must exist for the sake of people.

Emerson said that the purpose of religion is to make people "good and wise." I pointed out in my 1993 Harvard lecture what I believe are the criteria we must keep firmly in view:

> In an age marked by widespread religious revival, we need always ask: Does religion make people stronger, or weaker? Does it encourage what is good or what is evil in them? Are they made better and wiser by religion?[6]

Emerson likewise wrote in his journal on July 6, 1832:

> Religion in the mind is not credulity & in the practice is not form. It is a life. . . . It is not something else *to be got*, to be *added*, but is a new life of those faculties you have.[7]

These sentiments accord completely with the SGI's philosophy.

BOSCO: Although biographers and critics have said much about Emerson's views on religion, especially in the context of his resignation from the Second Church pulpit, in my view Emerson did not leave religion as such; instead, he simply replaced the religion of the pulpit with the humanistic and secular homilies he delivered from the lecture platform.

After leaving his ministry, Emerson slowly but steadily moved in the direction of taking on a new career as a writer and lecturer. It is interesting to me to recall the comments of Elizabeth Palmer Peabody, one of his oldest friends. In a lecture titled "Emerson as Preacher," she remarked that he was

> always pre-eminently the preacher to his own generation and future ones, but as much—if not more—out of the pulpit as in it; faithful unto the end to his early chosen profession and the vows of his youth.[8]

IKEDA: His faith was no mere formality. It was something inherent in him, something coming out of his own initiative, inseparable from his way of life.

MYERSON: Thinking of how faith should be, in my exchanges with them, I have felt that SGI members embody the best spirit of the American Renaissance.

IKEDA: Thank you for understanding our aims.

CONVERSATION NINE

Emerson Finds His Audience

A Chance To Reexamine Life

IKEDA: Though he knew she was ill when they married, Ellen's death must have caused Emerson immeasurable grief. He overcame it, however, and started out boldly on a new path in life.

In the process, he mastered the idea of "Compensation," the title of one of his essays published in a collection ten years after Ellen's death.

He wrote:

The death of a dear friend, wife, brother, lover, which seemed nothing but privation, somewhat later assumes the aspect of a guide or genius; for it commonly operates revolutions in our way of life, terminates an epoch of infancy or of youth which was waiting to be closed, breaks up a wonted occupation, or a household, or style of living, and allows the formation of new ones more friendly to the growth of character.[1]

Tragedy and suffering indeed provide us the chance to re-examine our lives and serve as guideposts for living in a deeper, stronger way.

BOSCO: During the 1830s and 1840s, four people close to Emerson died: Ellen; his brothers Edward and Charles; and little Waldo Emerson, Emerson's son by his second wife. Ellen, Edward, and Charles died of tuberculosis in 1831, 1834, and 1836, respectively; and Waldo died of scarlatina at five in 1842.

The deaths of these four persons were, indeed, times of great crisis and distress for Emerson. Their deaths were devastating for him, but as President Ikeda says and as the essay on "Compensation" reveals, they provided Emerson with a chance to reexamine life.

The loss of ones dear to him served Emerson as opportunities to seek guideposts for a new way of living. After Ellen's death and his resignation from the Second Church a year later, Emerson left Boston for an extended journey to Europe, thus expanding his view of the world. This journey also enabled him to reconcile himself to the tragedy of Ellen's loss.

IKEDA: My mentor's first child died at age one. In the fourth year of his first marriage, his wife died of pulmonary tuberculosis, and his doctor suspected that Toda had been infected with the disease.

Reflecting on that period, he said:

Never has the world been filled with such sorrow for me as it was then [when his daughter died]. One day at my office in Meguro, I thought to myself, "What if my wife were to die?" And that brought me to tears. And then my wife, too, died. Later I wondered what I would do if my mother died. I was, of course, very fond of my mother. Pursuing things still further, I shuddered at the thought of my own death.

While in prison during the war, I devoted some time to reading the Lotus Sutra. One day I suddenly understood; I had finally found the answer. It took more than twenty years to solve the question of death. I had wept all night over my daughter's death and dreaded my wife's death and the thought that I, too, would die. Because I finally could answer this riddle, I became president of the Soka Gakkai.[2]

I also understand the anguish of a parent whose child has died. I lost my second son.

Memento mori, as the Latin saying has it: "Remember that you, too, must die." By confronting the issue of life and death, we can understand our true selves and the meaning of life. This, to me, is what Emerson means by *compensation*.

POSING THE DIFFICULT QUESTIONS

MYERSON: I am especially drawn to Emerson because he posed difficult questions. After many years of studying him, I have come to feel that there are too many people who regard him not as one who asks questions but as a model who lives the answers.

For example, I cannot help thinking that many people read "Self-Reliance" less to deepen their ways of thinking for the sake of actually becoming self-reliant than as a kind of rulebook. We cannot understand the true meaning of *compensation*—to which President Ikeda just referred—without a thorough understanding of the life Emerson led.

IKEDA: Shakyamuni Buddha encouraged his disciples to question before accepting the Buddhist teachings. Socrates was likewise skilled at asking questions and initiating dialogue to dispel others' delusions and cultivate their wisdom. Emerson strove to awaken people to a better life through his lectures, which he took up seriously upon his return from overseas.

BOSCO: Two months after his return to Boston, Emerson wrote, "The call of our calling is the loudest call."[3] Having left the traditional "call" of the pulpit, he now became excited at the prospect of participating in the popular lyceum movement then sweeping America.

He saw that the lecture hall could serve him as a site of transition from the pulpit and afford him a congenial setting in which to test before large audiences his evolving thoughts on philosophy, literary history, nature, and the human condition.

IKEDA: Thus he started on his new path to educate the people with new ideas.

BOSCO: By 1835, he was writing and delivering multi-lecture series, the first of which was on the subject of biography and the second on English literature, both of which remained among Emerson's lifelong interests. The success of these series, along with Emerson's growing confidence as a writer, put him in control once more of his professional destiny and served him with the means to be reconciled to the loss of Ellen, Edward, and then Charles, who would die in 1836.

FINAL DAYS OF A "BALANCED SOUL"

MYERSON: During this time, Emerson formed friendships with many of the major literary figures of his day, such as Fuller and Thoreau, and lesser ones, such as Bronson Alcott. Also during this period, Emerson published many of his most famous works, for example, *Nature* in 1836. Through lectures like "The American Scholar" and the "Divinity School Address," he introduced new philosophical currents into the society of the time.

IKEDA: It was also during this time that Emerson and Whitman came in contact. In a letter to the poet, Emerson expressed the highest praise for a copy of *Leaves of Grass* Whitman had sent him:

I rubbed my eyes a little, to see if this sunbeam were no illusion; but the solid sense of the book is a sober certainty. It has the best merits, namely of fortifying and encouraging.[4]

These warm words must have encouraged Whitman, at the time unknown, reviled, and experiencing great difficulties.

Leaves of Grass was a source of tremendous spiritual nourishment for me as a struggling young man. The sentiments expressed in Emerson's letter remind me how I felt when I first obtained a copy of *Leaves of Grass* during the upheaval of the postwar period.

BOSCO: A later Emerson essay, "The Poet," celebrates the ideal poet as the one who "chaunt[s] our own times and social circumstance," who serves as the "reconciler," and who captures the "genius" of America in verse.[5] We do not have to look beyond Whitman's "Song of Myself" to see fulfilled one of Emerson's major requirements for the thinking man and for the poet—that, like Dante, they write their "autobiography in colossal cipher, or into universality."[6]

IKEDA: "Song of Myself" starts with the famous line "I celebrate myself, and sing myself."[7]

MYERSON: The publication of Emerson's first two volumes of essays, in 1841 and then in 1844, firmly established him as a major literary figure. In 1847–48, he visited Britain and gave a series of lectures to great acclaim.

A volume of *Poems* was published in 1847. In 1849, he published *Nature, Addresses, and Lectures* and *Representative Men*.

IKEDA: Triumphing over the loss of beloved family members, Emerson produced these great works one after another.

MYERSON: The next two decades were marked by many more successes. Emerson's lecturing career flourished, and his series on his visit to England was published in 1856 as *English Traits*.

But by the late 1860s, Emerson's health began to fail. A fire partially destroyed the Emerson house in July 1872, further accelerating his decline.

IKEDA: By then, he was sixty-nine, his health and memory deteriorating.

MYERSON: He and his daughter Ellen visited Europe and Egypt while the house was being rebuilt, but he was never the same after returning to Concord. Emerson died quietly in Concord on April 27, 1882, and was buried at Sleepy Hollow Cemetery, close to the graves of the Alcotts, Hawthornes, and Thoreaus.

IKEDA: The Sage of Concord, as he was known, died at seventy-nine. What were his last years like?

BOSCO: As most of his biographers agree, Emerson slowly descended into old age, which he accepted with the grace characteristic of one who had lived a full life and who, by adding to the native intellectual wealth of American culture, had done much good for his fellow citizens. Although his frail health during his last years was a great trial for those around him, in the following lines from "Terminus," which he published in 1867, he demonstrates to me that he consciously approached his end with complete equanimity:

> As the bird trims her to the gale,
> I trim myself to the storm of time,
> I man the rudder, reef the sail,
> Obey the voice at eve obeyed at prime:
> 'Lowly faithful, banish fear,
> Right onward drive unharmed;
> The port, well worth the cruise, is near,
> And every wave is charmed.'[8]

IKEDA: Emerson's deeply moving verse shows that, even as his body started to fail him, his spirit retained its vigor.

More than thirty years ago, returning to Paris from London after Arnold J. Toynbee and I had concluded our dialogue (published as *Choose Life*), my train passed through the Loire region, site of the French Renaissance. I stopped at the Château at Amboise, where Leonardo da Vinci spent his later years. In the room where he died, there was a bronze plaque bearing his words: "A well filled day gives a good sleep. A well filled life gives a peaceful death." Emerson's life and the timelessness of his work surely add up to what da Vinci meant by a "well filled life."

BOSCO: In light of the consistency—so evident in the lines of "Terminus"—with which Emerson lived the greatest portion of his mature life and accepted with gentle resignation the inevitability of its end, is it any wonder that to this day Emerson stands alone as America's premier spokesman for the ideal? He is, to my mind, the best representative of one of his own ideal constructions—the "balanced soul."[9]

CONVERSATION TEN

Nature, "The American Scholar," and the "Divinity School Address"

IKEDA: A writer's philosophy often finds its best expression in a writer's first work. I think this is true of *Nature*, which Emerson wrote when he returned from Europe.

BOSCO: *Nature*, which was published on September 9, 1836, is Emerson's sweeping declaration of the divinity of human life and the universality of thought. Having assimilated much from his readings in Platonic and neo-Platonic thought, in Eastern philosophy and religion, and in natural history, Emerson proclaimed nature the resource through which individuals can restore "original and eternal beauty"[1] to their world and achieve the redemption of their souls.

IKEDA: We earlier discussed (see Conversation Three) Emerson's opening passage:

> Our age is retrospective. It builds the sepulchres of the fathers. It writes biographies, histories, and criticism. The foregoing

generations beheld God and nature face to face; we, through their eyes. Why should not we also enjoy an original relation to the universe? Why should not we have a poetry and philosophy of insight and not of tradition, and a religion by revelation to us, and not the history of theirs?[2]

He was saying that instead of being satisfied with borrowed ideas and content with formalized faith, we should stand on our own two feet. In other words, we should live true to ourselves.

BOSCO: In the rousing opening lines, Emerson rejected idolaters and sepulchre-builders, the theological "Philosophes," who only reinforce the intellectual and imaginative stupor of their time. In their place, he proposed in his essay a new class of thinker and minister who will write as prophets and priests; who will, as he elaborated in "Compensation," create the "so dear, so sweet, so graceful"[3] through reference to the "force in Today" instead of reverencing the "ruins of the old tent"; who will look to "energy instead of limitation," to the metaphoric "Sea instead of the Shore."[4]

MYERSON: For the Transcendentalists of the time, because nature was a manifestation of the creative power of God, because God was immanent or present in nature, the study of nature became a study of God.

Emerson helped to shape the Transcendentalists' view of the natural world with the publication of *Nature*, at the beginning of which he posed the central question of the book: "Let us inquire, to what end is nature?"[5] His desire to know nature's purpose assumes that there is something behind what we see.

DELIGHT IN KNOWING THE WORLD

IKEDA: *Nature* expressed the oneness of nature and humanity in poetic terms. Thoughts inspired by field and forest prompted Emerson to write that he was not alone and ignored in such places.

The trees and flowers waved to him; he waved back. He emphasized delight in interacting with nature.

I find especially compelling his description of the source of such delight: "It is certain that the power to produce this delight, does not reside in nature, but in man, or in a harmony of both."[6]

BOSCO: The same idea is found in Eastern thought.

IKEDA: The Buddhist view of nature and the world is called *dependent origination*. This is the teaching that all phenomena are connected, and none exist independently. All things are joined in a great web of interdependent connections, which ultimately constitute the cosmos. True human happiness is born from expanding our awareness of this integration.

BOSCO: The concept is close to what Emerson called "correspondence."

In Paris in 1833, he spent an entire day at the Jardin des Plantes, wandering through the rooms of the Cabinet of Natural History, where he discovered for the first time in his life the relational nature of all things in the universe.

IKEDA: He probably experienced a kind of enlightenment resulting from his extended reflection.

BOSCO: Let me quote in their entirety Emerson's remarks on how that unique experience challenged, but also opened, his mind:

> Here we are impressed with the inexhaustible riches of nature. The Universe is a more amazing puzzle than ever as you glance along this bewildering series of animated forms—the hazy butterflies, the carved shells, the birds, beasts, fishes, insects, snakes—& the upheaving principle of life everywhere incipient in the very rock aping organized forms. Not a form so grotesque, so savage, nor so beautiful but is an expression of some property inherent in man the observer—an occult relation between the very scorpions

and man. I feel the centipede in me—cayman, carp, eagle, & fox. I am moved by strange sympathies, I say continually, "I will be a naturalist."[7]

IKEDA: The ideas contained here constitute the very structure of *Nature*. In "Prospects," the concluding section, Emerson wrote, "The reason why the world lacks unity, and lies broken and in heaps, is, because man is disunited with himself."[8] The problem of humanity's disunity with itself is increasingly grave today. It is growing harder for human beings to live up to the best of their capabilities.

MYERSON: Emerson believed that people use only half their powers: only their understanding. He asks us to look beyond things for their meaning, to go behind the surface for the cause. As this passage indicates, the world lacks unity because people are disunited with themselves; nature appears fragmented because people do not use their reason or intuition to see the unity in variety.

THINKING FOR OURSELVES

IKEDA: We have mentioned Emerson's advice from the conclusion of *Nature* to "build . . . your own world." He continued:

> As fast as you conform your life to the pure idea in your mind, that will unfold its great proportions. A correspondent revolution in things will attend the influx of the spirit.[9]

MYERSON: When people learn to listen to the spiritual part of themselves, they will see the goodness they discover there reflected in the natural world. When they use their reason correctly, they will see again. This is the message of the final chapter of *Nature*.

If *Nature* examined the world of the senses, then Emerson's next publication, "The American Scholar," an address delivered at Harvard commencement celebrations on August 31, 1837, examined the world of the mind. This oration set forth the duties and responsibilities of the American scholar, whom Emerson described as "Man Thinking."

BOSCO: In it, Emerson expanded on the themes of *Nature* and challenged America's future writers and professors to break with their dependence on imitation of classical and European models in their art and thought. Imitation, he argued, makes people and their intellects passive; he wanted, instead, active scholars, people of original thought who aspire to be something more than mere parrots of other people's words and ideas.

IKEDA: A nation frantic with building new things, the United States required new ways of thinking. At the beginning of "The American Scholar," Emerson stated, "Our day of dependence, our long apprenticeship to the learning of other lands, draws to a close."[10]

He insisted that the American scholar must be independent of European culture. The education of the scholar, he added, must be through nature, books, and taking action.

MYERSON: For Emerson, nature is important because it is the direct study of God, and, because nature is contemporaneous with us, we are studying God as being present in the world today. Books, on the other hand, are what Emerson called the "best type of the influence of the past."[11]

Unfortunately, human nature is such that it prefers assurances and securities to speculations and the unknown, and so it tries to find a single truth and hold on to it. Emerson presented us with a disturbing scenario, arguing that originality becomes tradition as the original thoughts of one generation are transformed into the texts that the next generation is made to memorize.

Emerson warned that, unless each generation tries to be original, tries to reinterpret the universe, we are doomed to replicate the past instead of moving forward. "Hence," said Emerson, "instead of Man Thinking, we have the bookworm."[12]

IKEDA: While recognizing the value of books, Emerson warned against believing everything you read. In "The American Scholar," he similarly cautioned against people who "start wrong, who set out from accepted dogmas, not from their own sight of principles."[13]

The same warning applies to youth today, who must bear the responsibility for coming generations. The inability to think for themselves makes people gullible to the deceit of power and authority, thus rendering people incapable of detecting and halting dangerous propensities in society.

Action, Emerson's third kind of education for the scholar, is the best way to generate the power to think for ourselves. "Action is with the scholar subordinate, but it is essential," he said. "Without it, he is not yet man. Without it, thought can never ripen into truth."[14] Contemporary intellectuals and scholars would do well to heed this counsel.

ALWAYS TRUE TO HIS BELIEFS

BOSCO: The scholar must be an active participant in the world and not isolated in a study. This message is indeed important today. In 1838, Emerson reinvoked "Man Thinking" to stir the imaginations of young ministers who were then graduating from Harvard Divinity School.

In religion, as in art, Emerson said, imitation cannot move beyond its models, so the imitator is doomed to hopeless mediocrity. Observing that the formalism of traditional Christian practices was a sign of a "decaying church and a wasting unbelief"[15] that left worshippers thoughtless, defrauded, and disconsolate, he urged his audience to become "newborn bard[s] of the Holy Ghost . . . [to] acquaint men at first hand with Deity"[16] and "rekindle the smouldering, nigh quenched fire on the altar."[17]

IKEDA: Six years before delivering this address, Emerson was in the following state of mind, captured in an October 9, 1832, journal entry:

I will not live out of me
I will not see with others' eyes . . .
I dare attempt to lay out my own road[18]

In the following, included in his "Divinity School Address," he drew from his own spiritual experience:

> Let me admonish you, first of all, to go alone; to refuse the good models, even those which are sacred in the imagination of men, and dare to love God without mediator or veil.[19]

MYERSON: The "Divinity School Address" warned of the dangers facing the increasingly conservative Unitarian church. The religion of the day, Emerson argued, had, through its emphasis upon Biblical miracles, changed people's view of Jesus Christ from that of a prophet who showed them the divinity within themselves to that of a remote demigod, far removed from their daily lives.

Likewise, ministers preached a historical Christianity that no longer inspired people. Emerson gave as an example of this a minister who preached so poorly during a snowstorm that the white flakes outside seemed more substantial than the words spoken within.

IKEDA: I understand that Emerson's lecture provoked a storm of criticism at Harvard, then a bastion of conservative Unitarianism.

MYERSON: The traditionalist Unitarians reacted vigorously against this address—the leading one, Andrews Norton, calling it the "latest form of infidelity"[20]—with the controversy spilling over into the daily papers and Emerson not being officially invited back to Harvard for nearly thirty years.

IKEDA: In letting them know what things were really like in the church, Emerson was expressing his wish that these future ministers would bring about a revival. He rejected many friends' advice not to publish the lecture and issued a limited edition.

Always true to his beliefs, he shared them as hope for the future, bowing to no authority. This attitude represents what I consider the prerequisite for a real philosopher, one capable of creating new currents for a new epoch.

An Intellectual Independence

BOSCO: *Nature,* "The American Scholar," and the "Divinity School Address" were great achievements in establishing American intellectual independence. The three can be called the foundation for Emerson's later interpretations of literature, morality, politics, and society.

IKEDA: These lectures opened the door on a new American age. In my first Harvard lecture, "The Age of Soft Power," I included some of Emerson's poetry. Responding to the lecture, Harvey Cox, a Harvard professor and leading theologian, reminded us that 150 years earlier Emerson had at Harvard sounded a warning to those ensconced in tradition and authority.

Dr. Cox said that true learning and knowledge must never be controlled by authority; they must gush forth from the inner life and experience of each individual.

He added that, in its attempt to revive inner-motivated philosophy in the current age, my lecture recalled the true meaning of Emerson's address. Dr. Cox's comments increased my awareness of Emerson's achievement.

MYERSON: In your annual peace proposals (published each year on January 26, the anniversary of the SGI's founding), you employ terms like *renaissance, horizons, challenge, dawn,* and *a new century* that, I am convinced, correspond to words employed by the Transcendentalist pioneers of the American Renaissance. Pulsating with the spirit of that Renaissance, your words indicate the present inapplicability of outmoded philosophies and the need to once again create something new.

CONVERSATION ELEVEN

Representative Men

THE "HOBGOBLIN OF LITTLE MINDS"

IKEDA: Dr. Bosco and Dr. Myerson, when you visited Soka University of Japan in 2001, you presented us with a precious edition of Emerson's *Nature*. Soka University has treasured the book, displaying it in the university's Central Tower. Let me thank you once again.

BOSCO: We are gratified that Emerson's work has attracted the attention of many Soka students and are grateful for your contribution to that.

IKEDA: Students continue to show great interest in Emerson. It is my wish that many will continue to be enlightened by *Nature*, which contains the roots of the American Renaissance. In *Nature*, "The American Scholar," and the "Divinity School Address," Emerson called on people to break through old-fashioned formality, look within themselves once again, and return to the origins of humanity to establish a new way of life.

MYERSON: Emerson's first volume of essays, published in 1841, included "Self-Reliance," which sets forth his belief that, since all people contain a spark of divinity, the nurturing of this divinity— by ignoring the conformist demands of society—results not only in self-reliance, but in God-reliance as well.

In "Self-Reliance," Emerson stated, "A foolish consistency is the hobgoblin of little minds,"[1] showing his conviction that our beliefs should reflect the constant change of never-static life. I am sure that, if he read it, Emerson would completely agree with what you said in your 2002 peace proposal: "Since the ultimate enemy is dehumanization, the ultimate solution must be a revitalization and restoration of humanity."[2]

IKEDA: You are too kind. My ideas aside, Emerson's philosophy is permeated with a thorough knowledge of humanity.

Let's next examine Emerson's views on humanity as expressed in *Representative Men*, a compendium of a series of lectures he gave in Boston and Manchester, England, beginning in 1849. He selected as representative of human history six figures: Plato, Emanuel Swedenborg, Charles de Montesquieu, William Shakespeare, Napoleon Bonaparte, and Johann Wolfgang von Goethe.

BOSCO: In *Representative Men*, Emerson created a distinct hierarchy, with the figures featured in the book representing various aspects of the heights to which humans have aspired and have achieved. Shakespeare, for instance, represents the highest expressions of poetic genius and artistic comprehension of the human condition.

Napoleon, on the other hand—even though he seems to lack certain ethical qualities that Emerson considered essential to being the fullest type of a "representative man"—is to Emerson an unparalleled example of democratic leadership and military genius.

IKEDA: Emerson based the style of *Representative Men* on Carlyle's *Heroes and Hero Worship*.

Though in some instances—Shakespeare and Napoleon, for example—the two authors deal with the same figures, their approach toward the idea of heroes differed fundamentally. Carlyle saw greatness in the heroes themselves; heroes are in possession of special strengths lacking in ordinary people.

Emerson, on the other hand, believed great strength to be inherent in everyone. He saw the six figures he chose as examples of those who manifested their strengths and brought them to fruition. The difference between the two books is apparent from their titles.

Emerson clarified his approach in the following passage from the essay "The Poet":

The breadth of the problem is great, for the poet is representative. He stands among partial men for the complete man, and apprises us not of his wealth, but of the commonwealth. The young man reveres men of genius, because, to speak truly, they are more himself than he is.[3]

Great people in history, who embody the best of their times, manifest the wealth—the humanity and spiritual strength—inherent in everyone. Beholding the natural genius of such people awakens others to their real strengths. I think the idea permeating Emerson's *Representative Men* is the dignity of all humanity.

BOSCO: In a journal passage written some years before his work on *Representative Men*, Emerson defined "little-endians"[4] as those persons from his everyday life who, although not traditionally great in the same way that, say, Shakespeare or Napoleon were great, nevertheless commanded his respect and admiration. ("Little-endians" is an allusion to the orthodox Lilliputians in Jonathan

Swift's *Gulliver's Travels*, who insisted that boiled eggs must be eaten starting with the little end.)

In his journal, he wrote, "The world looks poor & mean so long as I think only of its great men; most of them of spotted reputation." But he found inspiration in remembering "how many obscure persons I myself have seen possessing gifts that excited wonder, speculation, & delight in me. . . ."[5]

IKEDA: Who does "obscure persons" refer to? From my own experience—and the experiences of the SGI movement—I can say without hesitation that the nameless ordinary people create the undercurrent of history.

BOSCO: Emerson's "little-endians" were those people he met whose lives were "poems" and who represented the highest, "accomplished" company of his time and place.[6] Who were these people? They were Bronson Alcott, Mary Moody Emerson, Thoreau, Ezra Ripley, and others who were largely unknown in their time but have great significance for us.

He believed, for instance, that like Michelangelo, John Milton, and St. Augustine, such figures as Dr. Ripley and Thoreau possessed brains in which could be calculated the "geometry of the City of God,"[7] as he wrote in his essay "The Method of Nature." For him, like Socrates, St. Paul, and Shakespeare, such figures as Alcott and his Aunt Mary possessed hearts that served as the "bower[s] of love" and that provided them keys to the "realms of right and wrong." Finally, they were people who, for Emerson, reconfirmed his enchantment with the world and represented the truest form of democracy.[8]

SEEING OURSELVES IN OUR HEROES

MYERSON: Writers active in the American Renaissance like Hawthorne and Melville interpreted the possibilities of life in different ways. For instance, Hawthorne, who was greatly concerned with the individual in an oppressive society and the influence of the past on the future, could not sympathize with the sense of optimism inherent in Emerson's philosophy.

IKEDA: Melville adopted still another viewpoint.

MYERSON: Melville agreed with Emerson about the importance of the individual pursuit of truth. But the two differed about people's ability to grasp truth.

Melville was skeptical about human importance in relation to nature and about human ability to understand nature's lessons. In other words, whereas, like Emerson, he wanted to discover the truth, he felt human beings were blind to the great truths confronting them and incapable of understanding the most important lessons inscribed in nature.

IKEDA: In the "Divinity School Address," Emerson encapsulated his optimism: "He [Man] learns that his being is without bound; that, to the good, to the perfect, he is born, low as he now lies in evil and weakness." And later, in the same address: "He is religious. Man is the wonderworker. He is seen amid miracles."[9]

BOSCO: Those lines directly express Emerson's way of thinking.

IKEDA: Similarly, in a passage on Napoleon, Emerson wrote, "Every one of the million readers of anecdotes or memoirs or lives of Napoleon delights in the page, because he studies in it his own history."[10] Throughout *Representative Men*, Emerson was recommending not that we worship or pattern ourselves on his subjects but that we use them as mirrors to take a new look at ourselves.

BOSCO: In "Uses of Great Men," one of the most interesting, if neglected, chapters of *Representative Men*, Emerson wrote:

Once you saw phoenixes: they are gone; the world is not therefore disenchanted. The vessels on which you read sacred emblems turn out to be common pottery; but the sense of the pictures is sacred, and you may still read them transferred to the walls of the world.[11]

For a long time, I puzzled over this sentence—for two reasons.

IKEDA: What would those be?

BOSCO: First, I was unsure whether Emerson was likening the larger-than-life figures in the book to heroes or "phoenixes" whom we will never see again. Second, I was at a loss to reconcile Emerson's radical democratic views on the "infinitude of the private man,"[12] the breadth of human potential, with the sense he created in the book that the best men are always larger than life. After thinking about it for years, I came to the conclusion that the "little-endians"—the everyday people who, though not great in the traditional sense, nevertheless commanded his respect and admiration—provide the key to resolving the dilemma.

INDIVIDUAL REFORM AND SOCIAL REFORM

IKEDA: In fact, Emerson identified this idea of the "infinitude of the private man" as the "one doctrine" permeating all his lectures.[13] I believe that Emerson was concerned more than anything with helping people gain awareness of and bring to full flower their limitless potential. Such is exactly the aim of the SGI's movement for human revolution.

Buddhism teaches that the Buddha nature—the eminently noble state of life inherent in each individual—causes limitless spiritual power to flow forth. Such, in fact, is the goal of Buddhist faith. *Human revolution* means how, on a daily basis, to change not only oneself but society and the age as well.

MYERSON: It is your custom always to strive to know the position human beings occupy in the world and to understand their broad relationship with society. Of course, those relations entail many delicate problems.

Favoring the individual alone leads to egoism. Inclining toward society and seeking reputation can obliterate the individual.

Neither Emerson nor Thoreau was profoundly concerned about contributing to society. For one thing, they felt that social contributions must follow self-reformation. This is why they first set an example of how to live. This could then be propagated through publications to enlighten people on how to live in a meaningful way.

Your peace proposals and other publications have a similar value. But you have gone one step further to combine individual reform with social reform. The simultaneity of the two reforms in your approach is lacking in Emerson and Thoreau.

IKEDA: I take your words as an expression of your great expectations for the SGI's peace, culture, and education movement. Any attempt to build world peace that concentrates only on inner peace is in danger of lapsing into mere ideology or abstraction. True reform is achievable only through a movement in pursuit of expanded solidarity, global peace, and symbiosis.

Ultimately, however, both approaches are essential. We can generate the power to change our times only if we combine broad-scale activism with forging indestructible peace in the heart of each individual.

CONVERSATION TWELVE

The Inner Journey

SONGS IN PRAISE OF HUMANITY

BOSCO: The age of Emerson and Thoreau marks a distinct American literary response to the influence of the British Romantics of a generation earlier and a conscious endeavor to define America's original national character and vision through its literature.

IKEDA: English Romantic poets like William Blake, Percy Bysshe Shelley, John Keats, Lord Byron, and, to a lesser extent, William Wordsworth and Samuel Taylor Coleridge were all characteristically skeptical of modern society.

MYERSON: *Romanticism* was first used to describe writing that broke with the classical manner of the times; then it came to mean, in general, any type of innovative writing. Therefore, some prefer the term *American Romanticism* rather than *American Renaissance*.

BOSCO: As the terms were used at the time, *Renaissance* and *Romanticism* were concerned with not only literature and other intellectual fields but also with social reform, and in America the Renaissance and Romantic movements championed abolitionism, temperance, and women's rights. Moreover, as certainly evidenced by Thoreau, they greatly influenced the lives and values of environmentalists in that time.

IKEDA: Among the American Renaissance writers, some adopted a brighter and some a darker worldview and style. Emerson and Whitman, on the whole, represent the light. We see it in their confidence in the possibilities of every human being and their hopeful outlook toward the future. Hawthorne and Melville perhaps spent more time exploring the puzzling depths of human existence.

BOSCO: President Ikeda, your comments are the natural outcome of your consideration of the literature and intellectual concerns of Emerson, Thoreau, and Whitman, who have influenced you deeply. In your own poetry, especially *Songs from My Heart*, I feel that you share their orientation toward the light.

IKEDA: I believe that if a poet can perceive the infinite possibilities of humanity, his poetry naturally becomes a song in praise of humanity. The perception of those possibilities is really the perception of interconnectedness, like that between friends, between humanity and nature, and between humanity and the cosmos. Poetry crystallizes the surprise and emotion of awakening to such connections.

The Buddhist doctrine of dependent origination—again, the interdependence of all things—represents both a deep religiosity and poetic sensitivity.

"LIVES OF QUIET DESPERATION"

IKEDA: Where does the darkness in Hawthorne's work come from? I sense a religious influence.

MYERSON: Hawthorne was influenced by Calvinistic predestination and Puritan beliefs that our sojourn on Earth is but a temporary stop before eternal salvation or damnation. Calvinists saw human nature as evil because of original sin. In contrast, the Romantics and people associated with the American Renaissance regarded human nature as fundamentally good and, therefore, worthy of all possible opportunities for individual growth.

IKEDA: Thoreau kept a steady eye on both the bright and dark sides of American society and of humanity itself.

BOSCO: He perceived the dark aspects of human nature manifesting themselves in numerous ways, especially in his contemporaries' preoccupation with social convention and material wealth. He criticized these aspects of American life in *Walden*, when he wrote of the pitiful, desperate condition of so many of his fellow Americans:

> I see young men, my townsmen, whose misfortune it is to have inherited farms, houses, barns, cattle, and farming tools; for these are more easily acquired than got rid of. Better if they had been born in the open pasture and suckled by a wolf, that they might have seen with clearer eyes what field they were called to labor in.[1]

From this view of the everyday lives of his contemporaries evolves Thoreau's famous assessment of the human condition: "The mass of men lead lives of quiet desperation. What is called resignation is confirmed desperation."[2]

Thoreau's antidote to the "confirmed desperation" of his fellow men was the pursuit of a free and open life lived in concert with nature, such as the one he lived at Walden Pond.

IKEDA: Desperation narrows our field of vision and diminishes our vitality, thus leading to spiritual desiccation. Breaking out of our shells and taking the first courageous steps forward is the only way to escape desperation.

While living on Walden Pond, Thoreau was not really isolated from civilization. He came into contact with all kinds of people every day.

When townspeople visited and asked about his way of life, he answered them cheerfully. He even recalled how, "with the help of some of my acquaintances, rather to improve so good an occasion for neighborliness than from any necessity, I set up the frame of my house."[3]

BOSCO: Again, for Thoreau, closeness to nature can ameliorate the dark side of human nature.

IKEDA: Thoreau said, "I think that I love society as much as most."[4] No doubt, turning his gaze inward ultimately enabled him to discover the same expansive inner world in others.

At the end of *Walden*, he included this passage from the poem "To My Honoured Friend Sir Ed. P. Knight" by the English writer William Habbington:

> Direct your eye right inward, and you'll find
> A thousand regions in your mind
> Yet undiscovered. Travel them, and be
> Expert in home-cosmography.[5]

Each of the American Renaissance writers sought this inner world in his own way.

DRUNKENNESS IN DEGREES

BOSCO: At the end of his pursuit into the inner world, Thoreau discovered the fetters of civilization. He believed in the superiority of rustic over civilized or conventional life, with nature providing an inexhaustible source of inspiration and physical and mental health.

IKEDA: He tirelessly warned against becoming intoxicated with civilization and expressed his wish for sobriety: "I would fain keep sober always; and there are infinite degrees of drunkenness."[6] Many things beyond alcohol intoxicate human beings: money, fame, ideology, and so on.

Life in the forest distanced Thoreau from such intoxicants and taught him that viewing all things with a sober eye is essential. Touching on another kind of intoxication, Thoreau commented that "men have become the tools of their tools"[7] and that "our inventions are wont to be pretty toys, which distract our attention from serious things."[8]

Thoreau's words of caution for his own time have added gravity in our own.

BOSCO: In a December 11, 1855, meditation on his relationship with nature, Thoreau wrote:

> To perceive freshly, with fresh senses, is to be inspired.... My body is all sentient. As I go here or there, I am tickled by this or that I come in contact with, as if I touched the wires of a battery.[9]

One of my favorite "moral commands" from Thoreau was this: "Live in each season as it passes; breathe the air, drink the drink, taste the fruit, and resign yourself to the influences of each."[10] Surely this is an indispensable guide to maintaining sobriety in our daily lives and the quality of our interactions with other people.

IKEDA: The parable from the Lotus Sutra of the gem in the robe employs intoxication as a metaphor for human ignorance and its potentially harmful outcomes.

A poor man calls on a rich friend and drinks so much wine that he passes out. The rich friend, called away on an urgent matter, stitches an expensive jewel inside the sleeping man's robe. Awaking and finding his friend gone, the poor man sets out to make a living on meager earnings from whatever work he can find, totally ignorant of the treasure sewn into his garment.

After wandering from place to place, the poor man returns to his hometown and meets his rich friend once more. Astonished by the poor man's wretched condition, the rich man asks: "Why have you gone on suffering this way? I sewed into your robe a jewel worth enough for you to live comfortably on your whole life long."

It is the poor man's turn to be astonished. His friend reaches for the lining of the garment and says: "Look, it has been here all this time! And you have long suffered pain and overworked yourself because you did not know it."

Like the poor man in the story, many people live in unhappiness simply because they fail to realize that within their hearts they possess the pure, powerful Buddha nature.

Nichiren wrote, "The wine [in the story] stands for ignorance."[11] Intoxication here indicates a deluded life. The drunken eye can see only illusions.

Thoreau, however, learned to view reality with a sober eye. No doubt, he perceived a radiant jewel deep within all existence. Both Thoreau and the Lotus Sutra point to how human beings should live.

Questions Still To Be Answered

MYERSON: The American Renaissance came about at a time when various social and political forces were operating on the development of American culture, providing conditions and circumstances where people might be easily intoxicated. On the other hand, the growth of the frontier and the type of life that existed there, which was solitary in nature, resulted in people's valuing self-reliance and tolerating nonconformity, which, in turn, led to an appreciation of the American Renaissance authors, who questioned the established order.

BOSCO: In "The Rule of Life," a lecture he delivered in 1867, Emerson said that such devastating events as the Civil War and such positive events as the exploration of new lands in the American West were ultimately the "very stairs on which [the American] climbs" toward his realization of the ideal.[12]

IKEDA: All these currents flow toward the awakening of the American Renaissance. Emerson and Thoreau led the new tide. They asked whether humanity was losing sight of something important in the midst of all that industrial development.

Does wealth bring happiness? What is essential in life? What should be the real goal of democracy? All their questions still demand answers today.

BOSCO: Mid-nineteenth-century Americans harbored an ideal conception of their latent power for creating a great democratic society. Even though the particulars of each American's dream varied from one person to the next, I believe it is fair to say that Americans collectively dreamed of a great democracy—one that would transmute social power into higher forms of thought, provide for the moral and intellectual needs of humankind, take permanent political shape, and give new life to religion and art.

IKEDA: A major theme for the twenty-first century should be learning from and enhancing the luster of this American ethos. As Thoreau himself pleaded, "Be a Columbus to whole new continents and worlds within you, opening new channels, not of trade, but of thought."[13] It is my dearest wish that we can set out to these new continents under the rising sun of peace and coexistence.

Whitman's Original American Genius

THOREAU MEETS WHITMAN

IKEDA: Great souls magnetically pull one another closer until they meet, seemingly inevitably. This was true in the case of two giants of the American Renaissance, Thoreau and Whitman.

A poet of the people, Whitman's work was a companion to me in my youth. I still remember the thrill I felt when, in the impoverishment following the war's end, I scraped together the money to buy a translation of *Leaves of Grass*. Unlike most of the shoddy books of the time, it was handsomely bound and printed on good paper.

Whitman's poetry magnanimously affirms humanity and celebrates hope for a new age. This volume, which encouraged me more than I can say, was to me priceless.

BOSCO: A book from your youth that you have obviously treasured all your life.

IKEDA: I memorized some of my favorite verses and would sometimes recite them to myself as I made my way home late at night.

I understand that Thoreau visited Whitman in New York in 1856. Bronson Alcott accompanied Thoreau.

MYERSON: Thoreau and Alcott met Whitman in New York on November 10, 1856. As Alcott reported the meeting in his journal, Whitman met them "kindly, yet awkwardly."[1] The interaction between Thoreau and Whitman was strained.

IKEDA: In a letter, Thoreau frankly described his impression of Whitman:

> We . . . were much interested and provoked. He is apparently the greatest democrat the world has seen. . . . I am still somewhat in a quandary about him.[2]

MYERSON: Alcott added:

> Each seemed planted fast in reserves, surveying the other curiously,—like two beasts, each wondering what the other would do, whether to snap or run.[3]

IKEDA: It is often said that the first few minutes determine an encounter's success or failure. Tension is likely when two people of strong personalities and beliefs come together.

MYERSON: Thoreau commented in a November 1856 letter that Whitman possessed a "remarkably strong though coarse nature."[4] After reading *Leaves of Grass*, especially "Song of Myself," Thoreau commented in a December 1856 letter that "he has spoken more truth than any American or modern that I know" and that though "rude & sometimes ineffectual, it is a great primitive poem,—an alarum or trumpet-note ringing through the American camp."[5] Thoreau did have some problems with Whitman and his verse: "There are 2 or 3 pieces in the book which are disagreeable to say the least, simply sensual."[6]

IKEDA: Perhaps it was inevitable that a poet who proclaimed himself so proudly would puzzle Thoreau and other contemporaries. Whitman wrote, "I exist as I am, that is enough."[7]

IN TUNE WITH THE EAST

IKEDA: I believe that Thoreau and Whitman touched on Eastern literature in their meeting.

MYERSON: When Thoreau asked whether Whitman had read "the Orientals," the response was "No: tell me about them."[8]

IKEDA: Thinking of Whitman's poetic cosmos reminds me of the Buddhist scriptures. The canon is immense and took ages to build. But Nichiren expressed their fundamental core: "The storehouse of the eighty-four thousand teachings represents a day-to-day record of one's own existence."[9] He means that the scriptures describe the immense, profound world—or mental cosmos—within the individual: all its happiness, anger, sorrow, pleasure, hope, despair, courage, cowardice, justice, and evil. Thoreau, too, trained a powerful eye on the inner human cosmos.

BOSCO: Compelling comparisons.

IKEDA: For Nichiren, the example of one person represents the impartial truth inherent in all living beings.[10] Buddhism teaches the dignity and equality of life in all its forms. Using himself as the model, Whitman likewise sang of equality among all people.

BOSCO: I was born just a mile or two from Whitman's birthplace. That has always struck me as somewhat curious.

IKEDA: In what sense?

BOSCO: Because my career both as a teacher and a scholar has grown out of the influences of such people as Whitman and, of course, Emerson, in whose town, Concord, I now mostly live and will retire.

IKEDA: When, in June 1981, I visited the Long Island home where Whitman was born, it reminded me of my youthful days spent reading him. Morning glories bloomed around the simple house with its handsome trees and well-tended lawn. The three rooms on the first floor—sitting room, kitchen, and the room where Whitman was born—preserved the appearance of the past.

Such Whitman memorabilia as manuscripts, diaries, a portrait, a bust of Whitman in his later years, and a letter from Emerson were displayed in the two second-floor rooms. I remember the striking likeness between the Whitman bust—deeply lined face, prominent features, and flowing hair—and a bust of Leo Tolstoy I once saw in Moscow.

To the representative of the Walt Whitman Birthplace Association who was my guide, I said the house held much greater value than the skyscrapers of Manhattan. I expressed my great respect for the people who, loving and carrying on the poet's spirit, preserve and care for the house where he was born.

PRAISING EVERYTHING

IKEDA: Thoreau and Whitman were two entirely different types. In "Song of Myself," Whitman wrote:

Walt Whitman, a kosmos, of Manhattan the son,
Turbulent, fleshy, sensual, eating, drinking and breeding,
No sentimentalist, no stander above men and women or apart
   from them,
No more modest than immodest.[11]

He accepts and sings the praises of everything he finds in his life—the mixture of light and dark, good and evil, past and present. Here is the essence of his greatness.

MYERSON: At the end of "Song of Myself," he performed a virtuoso act that helped define his greatness as poet:

> Do I contradict myself?
> Very well then I contradict myself,
> (I am large, I contain multitudes.)[12]

In these lines, he gave a perfect poetic version of Emerson's statement that "foolish consistency is the hobgoblin of little minds."[13]

BOSCO: Whitman strikes me as the final, idealistic, poetic connection between the world of nature that Emerson theorized and that Thoreau initially put into practice. In Whitman's poetry, I find the completion of Emerson's theorizing on the nature of the poet most needed in America.

In poems like "Song of Myself" and his elegy on President Lincoln's assassination, I believe Whitman answered the complaint that Emerson articulated in "The Poet":

> The northern trade, the southern planting, the western clearing, Oregon, and Texas, are yet unsung. Yet America is a poem in our eyes; its ample geography dazzles the imagination, and it will not wait long for metres.[14]

IKEDA: Emerson wrote that the poet is "he who can articulate" the world.[15] The poet, he said, is thus "Namer" or "Language-maker."[16]

Nichiren likewise shared, "The sage observed the principles that govern [the various things in the world] and on that basis made up names for them."[17] Seeing things clearly, without prejudice, naturally enables you to praise them.

Emerson also wrote, "The poet names the thing because he sees it, or comes one step nearer to it than any other."[18]

ECHOES OF WHITMAN

MYERSON: The Transcendentalists all share the idea that the poet's role is to see the spiritual behind the actual, the higher laws behind the mundane facade of the world. To Emerson, for example, the poet functioned as a seer, someone who, by temperament and training, was better equipped than others to give expression to the natural world and the forces behind it.

IKEDA: These should indeed be the qualities of a poet.

MYERSON: The same thing can be said of both Thoreau and Whitman.

IKEDA: I believe that Thoreau ultimately came to hold a high opinion of Whitman.

MYERSON: Thoreau concluded, "He is a great fellow."[19] Surprisingly, Thoreau's visit seems to have made no impression on Whitman, who never mentions the occasion or Thoreau in any of his letters or journals.

IKEDA: What else should be noted about their connection?

MYERSON: When Whitman visited Emerson in 1881—nineteen years after Thoreau's death—he went to Walden Pond and placed a stone on the cairn at the site of Thoreau's cabin.

IKEDA: A touching conclusion.

BOSCO: To paraphrase Emerson, Whitman, like Dante, was the timely man, the great reconciler of conflicts and oppositions in the human condition, because he wrote "his autobiography in colossal cipher, or into universality."[20] Just as Thoreau is the Emersonian ideal living, experiencing, defining himself in nature, so Whitman is the Emersonian ideal of original American genius captured in and expressed through poetry.

IKEDA: Whitman could look candidly into his soul and scrupulously express it. At the same time, he extolled a universality accessible to everyone.

His is a song in praise of human life, an anthem to true democracy. His is a clarion trumpet call to a new century. The echo of his courageous poetic spirit rings through the years to summon us yet to pioneer new frontiers of the human spirit.

CONVERSATION FOURTEEN

The Boundless Potential of Life

EXPERIENCES IN EDUCATION

IKEDA: How fast time has flown! This August (2005) sees Soka University of America already welcoming its fifth class. In May, we proudly graduated our first class, giving a hundred students a glorious sendoff.

Though I was unable to attend, I was happy that people from around the world, including United Nations Under-Secretary-General Anwarul Karim Chowdhury and former president of the University of California Jack W. Peltason, were on hand to congratulate the graduates as they started the next chapter of their lives.

MYERSON: Time certainly does fly. We had the honor of visiting Soka University of America in May 2001, immediately before it opened, and were impressed by the mood of freedom and equality pervading the campus.

IKEDA: Thank you. And thank you, Dr. Bosco, for the substantive message of congratulations you sent the graduating class.

BOSCO: Because I had occasionally lectured there and interacted with students at all levels, I found the first Soka University of America graduation ceremony especially moving. For instance, after Professor Jim Merod asked me to share his classroom in 2004 and I had lectured on Emerson's life, I returned to Albany with the clear impression that all the students had prepared thoroughly, reading not only Emerson but Thoreau and Whitman as well.

It was also clear that they had seriously reflected on the intellectual relationships established among these three leaders of the American Renaissance. It occurred to me then that Emerson, who always enjoyed lecturing before audiences of college students, would have been moved by the sincerity of these students' desire to learn.

IKEDA: As Soka University of America founder, I appreciate your warm understanding.

I sent the graduating class a commencement message titled "The University of the 21st Century—Cradle of World Citizens,"[1] in which I argue that, in addition to intellectual concerns, education for the whole person, founded on global values and the philosophy of respect for all life, is going to be increasingly important. Offering this kind of education must be the overall mission and focal point of the university of the future.

BOSCO: I agree. Perhaps this provides us with a good transition into a discussion of Emerson's writings on educational reform.

IKEDA: For five years after graduating from Harvard, Emerson taught at a girls school run by his brother William. Emerson's journal reveals both his doubts about the educational system of the time and his efforts to do something about it.

MYERSON: When Emerson taught in schools—many of which were for young ladies—he had a limited young audience whom he was preparing for the next phase in their lives. For the young women, this may have meant further education, but that learning would have been more "practical" than intellectual in nature, focusing on things like housekeeping. For the young men, it meant preparing them for the rote education they would encounter at every future step on the academic ladder.

In the early nineteenth century, teaching was characterized by rote memorization intended to impose upon students a strictly defined world of knowledge. This approach resulted in the subordination of original, creative, and synthetic thinking to imitation and repetition. Emerson expressed his criticism of such education in "The American Scholar."

EMERSON'S ULTIMATE GOAL

IKEDA: Emerson's educational philosophy reached fruition in his lecture "Education," in which he warned that the "function of opening and feeding the human mind is not to be fulfilled by any mechanical or military method."[2]

Unfortunately, the overemphasis on accumulating knowledge alone persists today. Mere knowledge and information cannot make human beings happy or create social value.

BOSCO: Emerson enjoyed three careers: first, as a teacher in the early 1820s; second, as a Unitarian minister in the late 1820s and early 1830s; and third, as a lecturer from the mid-1830s to the end of his life.

I do not think it is helpful for us, however, to think of Emerson as enjoying *separate* careers as teacher, preacher, or lecturer. From my viewpoint, there is a dramatic consistency among Emerson's three careers, so much so that one could legitimately argue that the three activities formed one unified enterprise, the ultimate goal of which—from Emerson's perspective—was education.

MYERSON: Emerson strongly believed in using the lecture platform as a vehicle for making his audiences think. And there were plenty of outlets for lecturers in nineteenth-century America.

Learning was in vogue; and because not all people could read, the lecture was a popular method by which knowledge, thoughts, and messages were imparted. Emerson gave fifteen-hundred lectures over four decades.

IKEDA: Though we generally think of Emerson as contemplative and introspective, his forty years of lecturing suggest his openness to society in the role of educator and activist. I am especially impressed by the thorough, earnest preparation he made for each lecture as revealed by his journal.

He wrote that he never included things in his lectures that he had not thought about deeply. Nor did he speak on the spur of the moment. He felt that carelessly throwing together comments on a given topic was a waste of time for speaker and audience alike.[3]

All who heard him must have been moved by his deep contemplation, his unfeigned seriousness, and, most of all, his words, which poured forth from the innermost part of his personality.

LECTURES FROM THE HEART

BOSCO: Elizabeth Palmer Peabody was not alone among Emerson's contemporaries in her estimation of how his early careers as teacher and preacher influenced his interactions with friends and the public at large for the remainder of his life (see Conversation Eight). Annie Adams Fields, another longtime friend, remembered Emerson as one of those rare individuals who "warm and cheer us with something of their own beloved and human presences."[4] After hearing Emerson deliver a course of academic lectures titled "Natural History of the Intellect" at Harvard University in 1870, a student in the audience remarked, "[It] was not lectures to which we were listening, but poetry; not the teaching of the class-room, but the music of the spheres."[5]

IKEDA: Combining the poetry of nature and a paean to the inner life of human beings, Emerson's lectures must have been music to his listeners, moving them profoundly. Heart-to-heart resonance of this kind is indispensable to education.

Makiguchi had this to say:

> The technique—the art—of education entails supreme difficulties and cannot succeed without the very finest personnel. It has for its object the unsurpassed jewel of life, the most irreplaceable thing in the world. It is successful only when administered by people who embody both motherly and fatherly love.[6]

The term *unsurpassed jewel*, which appears in the Lotus Sutra, symbolizes the ultimate dignity of life. Makiguchi said that the educator is charged with the precious lives of children, with their limitless potential. The sacred work of education indeed requires that teachers devote their entire beings to their students. This idea is the kernel from which Soka education has grown.

BOSCO: Makiguchi's and your educational ideas have much in common with Emerson's philosophy and the methods toward which he strove to direct his students' and audiences' attention.

Emerson drew his students' and listeners' attention not only to the boundless potential of life in general but also to the limitless potential of which they were individually capable. I believe that Emerson's major contribution to his times as an educator was his elevation of his contemporaries' vision of the world and their place in it and his creation in them of a sense of self-confidence—a recognition, if you will, of their "self-reliance." Emerson's words and thoughts elevated the world around him, so much so that those who heard him and absorbed his thought felt themselves similarly elevated.

"FIRE OF THOUGHT"

MYERSON: Emerson always believed that the main educational function of his lectures was to cause people to think about themselves and major philosophical issues. In a similar fashion, you, President Ikeda, recognize the importance of inner growth to the message being delivered. In the "Divinity School Address," Emerson argued that the "capital secret" of the minister's profession is to "convert life into truth. . . . He deals out to the people his life,—life passed through the fire of thought."[7]

Teachers who are responsible for the happiness and future of their young charges should always bear these words in mind.

IKEDA: Dewey was deeply influenced by Emerson's ideas on education. In *The Child and the Curriculum*, Dewey wrote:

> Not knowledge or information, but self-realization is the goal. To possess the world of knowledge and lose one's own self is as awful a fate in education as in religion.[8]

Makiguchi, a contemporary of Dewey, insisted that happiness is the goal of education. Happy people, he believed, are strong and contribute to society.

In *Education for Creative Living*, his book on Soka education, he put it like this:

> The aim of education is not to transfer knowledge; it is to guide the learning process, to put the responsibility for study into the students' own hands. It is not the piecemeal merchandizing of information; it is the provision of keys that will allow people to unlock the vault of knowledge on their own. It does not consist in pilfering the intellectual property amassed by others through no additional effort of one's own; it would rather place people on their own path of discovery and invention.[9]

THE NATURE OF TRUE LEARNING

MYERSON: The more I hear of them, the closer Makiguchi's educational ideas seem to Emerson's. I am ashamed to say that, at one juncture, I was made painfully aware that I should have learned more from Emerson on the subject before I began teaching.

I had a rude awakening when I arrived at the University of South Carolina. For my first few years there, I was foolish enough to confuse programming students with educating them. Like most new teachers, I took shelter behind formal lectures. They were safe, but results were wretched.

IKEDA: In what way?

MYERSON: Students copied down what I said. With educational survival skills sharper than I gave them credit for, they quickly realized that, as long as they copied my words down, there was no need to think about them or be intellectually daring during class.

Naturally, they stopped reading books as thoroughly as they might have—or even reading them at all—because it was more important to memorize their class notes than to think about the texts. So I got smart and tried a new method of instruction.

IKEDA: What you had been doing amounted to force-feeding them information?

MYERSON: Yes. In a sense, after drawing up a road map for the class, over the course of a semester, I gripped the steering wheel of the car in which my students were passengers and ruthlessly drove them down roads I had marked as providing the best views.

No side trips were permitted, no interruptions allowed in the trip I had carefully planned. There was no reason for any intellectual give-and-take during the course.

So when this failed to produce results, I changed my method and started an unstructured discussion of the texts by encouraging the students to participate fully. Students' spirited discussions about their interpretations gave me new ideas about reading the texts, ideas that I incorporated into my scholarship and teaching.

Students actually read the assigned books so that they could participate in the free exchange of ideas that now marked my classroom philosophy. So finally, like Emerson, I came to realize that my role as a teacher was not to fill students up as empty vessels but to enable and empower them to think.

IKEDA: Your experience offers a practical lesson for us all. In East and West alike, instead of pushing students to merely accumulate information, the education system must put knowledge to good use by cultivating wisdom. In other words, knowledge should be a power source for human happiness and social accord. Soka education strives for this based on the Buddhist philosophy of awakening the wisdom of all people.

Makiguchi believed firmly Alfred Nobel's contention that though property can be inherited, happiness cannot.[10] We all possess boundless capability to create happiness for ourselves and others.

Human education promotes ways of living that make this creative act possible. I am convinced that this is the path education must follow in the twenty-first century.

CONVERSATION FIFTEEN

Thoreau's "Highest of the Arts"

How To Teach "Self-Culture"

IKEDA: Thoreau, like Emerson, started teaching after graduating from Harvard. In *Walden*, he wrote that he and his peers had "no school for ourselves. We spend more on almost any article of bodily aliment or ailment than on our mental aliment."[1] Also like Emerson, he was critical of a society that had no time to consider the nature of schooling or to understand what true education might be.

MYERSON: Emerson is reputed to have once said that most of the branches of learning were taught at Harvard College, to which Thoreau supposedly replied, "Yes, indeed, all the branches and none of the roots."[2]

IKEDA: The roots of education are indeed the most important thing.

Thoreau got a job teaching at the Concord Centre School but, opposed to corporal punishment, quit after only two weeks. His conscience could not countenance beating students in the name of discipline. It was alien to his idea of education.

Makiguchi strongly advocated the abolition of the prevailing system of classroom control and unwarranted interference in his time. Concerned primarily with children's happiness, he originated numerous school reforms. But suspecting he would deviate from the official policies, the authorities put pressure on him both openly and covertly.

This is why, in *Education for Creative Living*, he insisted on the need for schools' autonomy. In keeping with his aims, I advocate adding to the three basic human rights a fourth—the right to independence in education.

BOSCO: Your addition is an important one. As you rightly observe, Thoreau was impatient with the traditional classroom and rejected many of the traditional pedagogical methods of his time, especially corporal punishment. Neither the classroom nor the practices that teachers employed in 1830s, 1840s, or 1850s America were useful to Thoreau, whose subject was always the self in relation to nature, whose aim was always to teach "self-culture," and whose measure of success in teaching "self-culture" was invariably to see whether one's conscience—not one's bank account or standing in the community, for instance—grew with one's accumulation of knowledge.

We should, however, note that while Thoreau may have rejected traditional means of teaching and learning, he was nevertheless a true champion of education.

Cultivation of the Whole Individual

IKEDA: Thoreau had his own outstanding ideas on education. The year after his resignation, he and his brother, John, opened a private school in their home.

Their method was based on Bronson Alcott's idea of educating the whole person. After only three years, however, the school closed when John became ill. Nonetheless, I believe it must have been far ahead of its time.

BOSCO: Thoreau's adaptation of Bronson Alcott's education for the whole person included not only the inherited wisdom of the ages but also practical matters, such as farming, fishing, and hunting, independent reading and writing, the ideal way to commune with nature by immersing oneself in nature, and the importance of solitude as the perfect complement to society.

IKEDA: My mentor once ran a private school called the Jishu Gakkan, which, far transcending the conventional educational system, made liberal use of Makiguchi's philosophy of Soka education. In turn, I have founded educational institutions from kindergartens to the post-graduate level in hopes of preserving and putting into practice Makiguchi and Toda's humanistic educational philosophy, thus nurturing people who can contribute to lasting world peace and the happiness of all humanity. Soka education, like Bronson Alcott's system, strives to cultivate the whole individual.

MYERSON: What you say suggests a tide of value-creating education extending from Soka University of America to the whole world. Bronson Alcott was a self-taught Connecticut farmer's son who became the only man lacking formal education or Harvard connections to become one of the protagonists of the Transcendentalist movement.

Today, it is surprising to realize that the educational reforms he proposed to his contemporaries were then considered controversial: for instance, teaching in light and airy classrooms with comfortable furnishings, employing Socratic question-and-answer discussions, allowing students to arrive at knowledge on their own rather than having it spoon-fed to them, and students keeping journals in which they wrote down their ideas. His daughter Louisa May Alcott produced an idealized portrait of her father's schoolroom efforts in her fictional Plumfield School in *Little Women* and *Little Men*.

IKEDA: Though the progressiveness of his educational ideas earned him much misunderstanding from the general public, Bronson Alcott had the profound sympathy of intellects like Emerson and Thoreau. That Thoreau put Alcott's ideas into practice indicates his strong desire for a new kind of school, a new kind of education.

LIFELONG LEARNING FOR ALL

IKEDA: Thoreau's conviction rang out in this passage from *Walden*:

> It is time that we had uncommon schools, that we did not leave off our education when we begin to be men and women. It is time that villages were universities, and their elder inhabitants the fellows of universities, with leisure—if they are indeed so well off—to pursue liberal studies the rest of their lives. Shall the world be confined to one Paris or one Oxford forever? Cannot students be boarded here and get a liberal education under the skies of Concord?[3]

BOSCO: That is one of my favorite passages from *Walden*. It is a passage that reveals Thoreau's critique of education and its relation to learning in the nineteenth century and provides an alternative view of education.

The educated person, for Thoreau, was the person for whom the act of learning ended only with death. Further, to his way of thinking, the educated person always appreciates the fact that the accumulation of knowledge carries with it certain ethical responsibilities, not the least of which is to live up to the Socratic ideal of knowing oneself and, through knowing oneself, to leave the world better than one first found it. If there is any lesson he would have had his contemporaries take from his teachings, this is it.

IKEDA: Thoreau's belief that the truly educated person never loses the desire to learn corresponds with Makiguchi's insistence on lifelong learning.

The foundation of the American Renaissance was the grass-roots cultural and educational lyceum movement, with branches in about three thousand locations. Aimed at children as well as adults, lyceum lectures played a big part in the spread of democratic education.

The direct approach he adopted toward his lyceum audience we also see in Thoreau's prose style. I understand that people enjoyed hearing about his life on Walden Pond and his experience in jail.

MYERSON: Learning was popular in nineteenth-century America. Because not everyone was literate, lectures were an essential means of transmitting knowledge to the masses. Both Emerson and Thoreau served on the committee running the Concord lyceum.

Thoreau was asked to lecture some seventy-five times over a twenty-three-year public speaking career. Among his topics were "An Excursion to Cape Cod," "Slavery in Massachusetts," "Moonlight," "An Excursion to the Maine Woods," as well as a number of lectures on John Brown and a series drawn from the manuscript of *Walden*.

Reviews of his lectures were generally favorable, though some writers complained that they lacked system or organization. Generally speaking, his lectures about the natural world were preferred to those on other topics.

The Poetic Heart of Education

IKEDA: The following thoughts from Sophia Hawthorne, Nathaniel Hawthorne's wife, give us an idea of the immediacy of Thoreau's talks:

> His lecture before was so enchanting; such a revelation of nature in all its exquisite details of wood-thrushes, squirrels, sunshine, mists and shadows, fresh, vernal odors, pine-tree ocean melodies, that my ear rang with music, and I seemed to have been wandering through copse and dingle![4]

In "Life without Principle," Thoreau focused on the importance of speaking of deep inner things rather than merely skimming the surface. His manner of speaking was educational, moving listeners because his convictions arose from his experiences.

Different from ordinary schools in the eyes of Emerson and Thoreau, the lyceum circuit provided a broader field for human cultivation and education. They remind me of SGI activities.

BOSCO: In what way?

IKEDA: Throughout the SGI, we hold regular small discussion groups, where people come together to talk about their troubles or share their experiences of practicing Buddhism. They also discuss the teachings of Buddhism, the philosophy of peace, and various social themes.

The SGI promotes its grassroots movement for peace, culture, and education by encouraging people to engage in stimulating dialogue. Another important undertaking is our public seminars on peace, education, the environment, human rights, and health.

BOSCO: All are important activities. Thoreau was a poet of the mind and heart, for whom knowledge was accumulated not by rote but by entering daily into communication with the world of nature all around him. In *Walden*, in essays such as "Walking," and throughout his journal, he is the person of learning that you, President Ikeda, envisioned in a poem:

> Poetry is the heart that binds together human beings, society and the universe
> The poet's gaze fixes on the heart
> He does not see things as mere things
> At times the poet speaks with the grass and trees
> converses with the stars
> exchanges greetings with the sun
> Companion to all things
> he spies out their life force, breathes into them

penetrates the ever-shifting phenomena
of the real world
He fixes his eyes on the changeless laws of the universe[.][5]

IKEDA: I am convinced that restoring the spirit of poetry can restore education, thus becoming the driving force to enable students to win true happiness on their own.

BOSCO: With nature as his classroom, having developed for himself a poet's sensibility in interacting with nature all around him, Thoreau, I believe, could discover a world of knowledge that, as he said, was itself "so sanative, so poetic."[6]

IKEDA: Thoreau thought education should never be separate from the real world, the social environment, daily life.
    Dewey likewise warned:

Things hardly come within his (child's) experience unless they touch, intimately and obviously, his own well-being, or that of his family and friends.[7]

The belief that education should not be a preparation for life but an intimate part of life inspired Makiguchi to develop what he called the half-day school system. He insisted the educational ideal was for children to spend half the day in school and the other half in meaningful work, like learning a trade or practical skills.

DECIDING THE FUTURE

BOSCO: In "Serving the Essential Needs of Education," you wrote:

Learning is the very purpose of human life, the primary factor in the development of personality, that which makes human beings truly human. Nevertheless, development of personality has consistently been reduced to a subordinate position and viewed as a means to other ends.[8]

This passage succinctly captures the one great fear about the potential for the progress of human culture through education that both Emerson and Thoreau shared. Their fear was that education would degenerate into a means so that the joy of learning, like the joy and exuberance felt in experiencing oneself alive to the glorious influences of an unexpectedly early spring day, would be lost.

The challenges that face modern education are not new. What makes them significant today is the complexity of the world in which we live and the difficulty of leaving our world better than we found it, when so much seems poised to undermine our humanity through terrorism and war or to remove forever the source of poetry in life by our times' continuous plundering of the environment.

If these negative events prevail, then, I am afraid, Emerson— and, for me, especially Thoreau—will have lived in vain. I cannot accept that. We must take their most valued lesson to heart; that is, to cherish the diversity, which is the divinity, of the individual.

MYERSON: The key to resolving the educational crisis is to be found in the principles you set forth at the founding of Soka University in 1971:

For what purpose should one cultivate wisdom?
May you always ask yourself this question.

Only labor and devotion to one's mission give life its worth.

What these two directives share is a belief that the individual persists in developing and that education is continuous and never-ending.

At the same time, these goals urge us, once we have attained a sense of who we are and what we can accomplish, to use these skills to better the world around us and to work for world peace. In many ways, all of this was summed up by a question I was once asked by a student at one of the schools you founded: "How may I be a better person?"

IKEDA: As Soka schools founder, I am grateful for your words.

In the *Walden* chapter "What I Lived For," Thoreau wrote, "I know of no more encouraging fact than the unquestionable ability of man to elevate his life by a conscious endeavor."[9] And, later in the same chapter, "To affect the quality of the day, that is the highest of arts."[10] Thoreau's "highest of the arts" is a synonym for true education.

I have discussed education with many concerned world leaders who regard it as essential to the future of humanity. My conviction is that, although politics and economics are important, it is essentially education that determines the future.

I have the greatest respect for the two of you, heirs to Emerson and Thoreau, heirs to the driving power of the American spirit. Seeing universal value in education, I strongly hope we can open new prospects for an educational renaissance in the twenty-first century.

CONVERSATION SIXTEEN

Bonds With Nature

DISASTERS ON THE RISE

IKEDA: Let me express my sorrow over the tremendous damage done by the powerful Hurricane Katrina (in August 2005). My condolences to all the families of the victims. I offer my deepest prayers that the region recover as quickly as possible.

BOSCO: As always, thank you, President Ikeda, for your kind sentiments and, especially on this occasion, for your prayers on behalf of the victims of Hurricane Katrina. There is no small irony in the fact that, as we have engaged in these lively conversations on the philosophy and positive views of nature shared among Emerson, Thoreau, Whitman, and others, we have witnessed two natural catastrophes in different corners of the world: the Asian tsunami that struck in December 2004 and now Hurricane Katrina.

As we speak, there are literally hundreds of thousands of people dislocated throughout the South. As in Sumatra, families have been torn apart in Louisiana, Mississippi, and Alabama, and many wonder if they will ever be reunited with their loved ones. Whole communities, along with their unique cultures and long-standing local traditions, have been literally wiped off the face of the map, and daily, it seems, the death toll mounts and mounts.

IKEDA: Katrina has been one of the worst disasters in United States history. The number of such calamities is increasing year by year throughout the world. According to some data, victims of natural disasters—including floods, droughts, heat waves, and cold snaps—rose from 720 million in the 1970s to 1.8 billion in the 1990s. During the three years between the start of 2000 and the end of 2002, the figure had already reached 1.2 billion for the current decade.

BOSCO: These are sad and alarming statistics with which we are becoming more and more familiar each year. Some people who are more cynical about nature than Emerson, Thoreau, or Whitman could ever have been are asking aloud whether nature is now betraying humankind.

But I think if these three figures were to walk among us today, they would ask us, "Is it not the case that humankind, not nature, is the culprit here?" Put another way, I would ask on their behalf, "Have we, as a global society, done everything within our power to protect the natural environment with which we all were originally blessed?" Regretfully, I think not.

For instance, global warming, which is an effect of negative human interaction with the natural environment, is one of the environmental changes already affecting our daily lives.

WANGARI MAATHAI AND THE GREEN BELT MOVEMENT

IKEDA: Global warming is believed to be the cause of various worldwide calamities, triggering abnormal conditions like the glacial lakes flood threat in the Himalayas. In February 2005, the Kyoto Accords, an attempt on the part of industrialized nations to mandate reductions in emissions of greenhouse gases, went into effect.

By the way, I had the chance to meet Wangari Maathai, Kenyan assistant minister in the Ministry of Environment, Natural Resources, and Wildlife, when she visited Japan for ceremonies to commemorate the Accords.

MYERSON: For her work with the Green Belt Movement, which has resulted in the planting of 30 million trees in Africa, she became the first African woman to receive the Nobel Peace Prize.

IKEDA: Maathai started by planting seven trees in her garden. Then many other women rallied round her to address Kenya's environmental problems and promote sustainable development.

Her path was treacherous. People in power who sought to profit from felling forests threatened her. She was imprisoned on several occasions and even tortured.

"If you want to change something, you must start by changing yourself," she told me. "Life is a wonderful experience. We should enjoy it." Her smiling face and earnest manner evidenced the strength and indomitable optimism of a mother who protects life.

BOSCO: The Green Belt Movement is one of the most important examples of responsible, enlightened environmentalism today. It accords precisely with the great thought of American and British Romantics who saw the need to replenish nature in order to protect the divinity of the individual. It is in the tradition of, especially, Thoreau's followers John Muir—the founder of the Sierra Club and advocate for America's national parks—and John Burroughs.

IKEDA: John Muir is known in Japan as the father of American conservationism. He and his friend the naturalist John Burroughs, a prolific author, were both influenced by Emerson and Thoreau, whose thought they inherited. They in turn exerted a tremendous influence on society.

BOSCO: In a global society, their view expands to include all nations, whose merit today and in the future will be measured by the care invested in protecting the environment.

IKEDA: Yes, nations and societies will be judged on how well they protect the environment.

LOSING THE WORLD, FINDING OURSELVES

IKEDA: It is sad that the natural environment is not what it once was anywhere—including in Tokyo, which used to be surrounded by nature. The Japanese author Kunikida Doppo described the natural beauty around Tokyo in his *Musashino* (1898):

> People should not distress themselves at getting lost, for wherever you go, there is something worthwhile to see, hear and feel.[1]

Kunikida's outlook corresponds to Thoreau's at Walden. Unfortunately, the scenery Kunikida loved has been almost entirely lost.

MYERSON: That passage from *Musashino* is virtually a mirror image of what Thoreau said in the "Village" chapter of *Walden*:

> Not till we are lost, in other words, not till we have lost the world, do we begin to find ourselves, and realize where we are and the infinite extent of our relations.[2]

IKEDA: Thoreau's "lost" seems to mean leaving behind a stereotypical life and stepping into a new world. Without being trapped in the established framework of modern civilization, we should reexamine the vast world of nature with a fresh eye.

BOSCO: From Thoreau's point of view, all the world has to be seen as a Walden in which, no matter where we turn in our walks through life, there—if we are attentive to nature—we will find knowledge and gain insights that bring us closer to the truth about ourselves and our relationship to nature.

MYERSON: Thoreau said that having found nature, we can lose "the world," which he defined as the social order, and, having lost society, we can then and only then find our *selves*, who we are. And when we find our selves, when we achieve a type of self-realization and self-actualization, only then can we discover our relationship to the world, both natural and social. This is, of course, much like the SGI's concept of value-creating education.

This, in turn, ties into the relationship between the human spirit and the destruction of the natural environment. To Thoreau and the Transcendentalists, nature is divine. Nature and humankind are both manifestations of the creative power of a higher deity, and as a result both are divine. Thus, when we destroy the natural world, we act in a sacrilegious manner.

IKEDA: Buddhism teaches that the individual and the environment constitute an inseparable, mutually influential unity. It also holds that universal life courses through all things—animate and inanimate. All things are endowed with the supremely precious, radiant Buddha nature. This means that to destroy the environment is tantamount to self-destruction, a view matching Thoreau's.

BOSCO: If there is one lesson I have drawn from my readings in Emerson and Thoreau, it is this: There are no shortcuts to immersing oneself in nature and, through that immersion, to discovering the divinity within ourselves. Writing in his journal on September 7, 1851, about his practices as a walker through nature, Thoreau defined his "profession" as "to be always on the alert to find God in nature, to know his lurking places, to attend all the oratorios, the operas in nature."[3] This was the posture he assumed throughout his time at Walden Pond.

IKEDA: Casually strolling through nature does not always enable us to sense its sacred rhythms. The important thing now is for the unclouded eye of the heart to perceive nature and discern the negative impact of humankind.

MYERSON: Thoreau looked deeply into both nature and civilization.

THE GLOBAL IN THE LOCAL

IKEDA: Kunikida wrote *Musashino* when Japan was undergoing modernization. As urbanization gradually increased, he must have, with a poet's keen eye, foreseen the environmental losses that modernization would cause.

Born the same year as Kunikida, Makiguchi sought the optimum path for human life in the face of said modernization. In his *Geography of Human Life*, he studied the influence geography and the natural environment exert on people.

MYERSON: A fascinating and thought-provoking topic. In connection with nature, Thoreau believed that the geography of the natural world had deteriorated into facts and figures to be memorized.

Too often the natural histories of the time were filled with Latinate names for species and columns of figures about them, giving no sense of the animals or plants themselves. Thoreau observed the natural world just as closely as did these scientists, but he saw in nature a new geography, one in which he could use plain terminology and his observations could be applied to daily life.

IKEDA: His ideas and Makiguchi's come together in a wonderful way. Makiguchi made the study of local culture the foundation of primary education. This begins with studying the relationship between a locale and local lifestyles, gradually expanding to study the region, the nation, and the whole world.

Studying the place where we live reveals its ties to the world and enables us to see the global embodied in the local. We learn that everything we eat and wear is bestowed by the world. This is how to create a field of learning that connects the local and universal.

MYERSON: Such a field of learning points the way to the conviction that all parts of the world are interdependent and that no nation can prosper unless all coexist in peace.

IKEDA: This relates to Thoreau seeing the world and the whole universe in Walden Woods.

BOSCO: Thoreau's world was, of course, the seemingly limited environs of Concord; however, for one who once said of himself that he was proud of having traveled widely in Concord, Thoreau inhabited a world that was anything but limited. Opening himself to all natural influences in the rural landscape around him, an environment in which he felt himself "God-propped" and "whole and entire,"[4] he thought himself rewarded with a world "gilded" for his delight.[5]

OPENING THE DOORS OF OUR HEARTS

IKEDA: Walden formed Thoreau, and he in turn made Walden more appealing. Indeed, the bonds between human beings and the land are unbreakable.

BOSCO: Observation of those bonds requires the sensitivity of a poet. In a journal entry for August 21, 1851, Thoreau wrote:

> What a faculty must that be which can paint the most barren landscape and humblest life in glorious colors! It is pure and invigorated senses reacting on a sound and strong imagination. Is not that the poet's case? The intellect of most men is barren. They neither fertilize nor are fertilized. It is the marriage of the soul with Nature that makes the intellect fruitful, that gives birth to imagination.[6]

He also wrote:

> There is some advantage, intellectually and spiritually, in taking
> wide views with the bodily eye and not pursuing an occupation
> which holds the body prone. . . . Granted that you are out-of-doors;
> but what if the outer door *is* open, if the inner door is shut![7]

IKEDA: I, too, believe that the scenery we behold can look entirely
different depending on whether the doors of our hearts are open or
closed. As Nichiren teaches, "It is the heart that is important."[8]

Outstanding thought and philosophy open these doors wide to
the abundance of nature and to other people. This points to the
great significance of teaching the work of American Renaissance
writers like Emerson and Thoreau in the classroom.

BOSCO: Emerson, Thoreau, and others of their generation are
indeed essential writers to include in all levels of education but
especially in those courses in which students are being introduced
to the relationship between themselves and their environment. No
matter what American literature course I teach, Thoreau's *Walden*
is always required reading along with Whitman's "Song of Myself" for their respective views of organicism. Thoreau certainly
teaches the value of an individual life well-lived in concert with
the environment, while Whitman teaches that the greatest value
an individual enjoys is the sense of belonging to a community of
individuals that is larger than himself alone.

CONVERSATION SEVENTEEN

Nature, Healing, and Health

EMERSON MEETS MUIR

IKEDA: For the dedication of the Soka University of America campus, I asked that one of the school's guiding principles be to "foster leaders for the creative coexistence of nature and humanity."[1] The hope that our students, leading the way as global citizens in the twenty-first century, would love nature and be environmentally conscious was one of the reasons for selecting a beautiful natural setting for Soka University of America. The bright, expansive Southern California environment plays an important role in the students' growth.

Young people visiting from Japan are immediately struck by the vastness of the United States—especially by the scale of the Grand Canyon, their favorite among the stunning national parks of the West, which include Yosemite, Sequoia, and Bryce Canyon.

BOSCO: It impresses me, too. I have visited many national parks in America's Northeast and far West, but my favorites have always been those coastal national parks such as the Cape Cod National Seashore, where looking out to the sea while standing on the shore I feel as though I am being swept out into the incomparable horizon. It is a feeling that has lasted since childhood, when my grandfathers and I walked along Long Island's Atlantic shore, and I wondered what worlds lay hidden beneath the breakers and beyond them past the horizon.

MYERSON: Those parks offer a contemplative retreat from the workaday world. My parents, however, never visited national parks because they found them boring: nothing to do there—no shopping, movies, and the like.

IKEDA: Muir devoted himself to the designation of the Grand Canyon as a national park. In 1960, I visited Muir Woods National Monument. I remember walking among the dense Coast Redwoods near San Francisco as wind rustled the needles of the trees, refreshing me—as if my life itself was being washed clean.

MYERSON: That must have been an exhilarating experience. Redwood forests once covered much of the Northwest.

But pioneers felled many of them for building materials. The forests of huge redwoods near San Francisco became a national monument in 1908.

IKEDA: Muir sounded the alarm on the environmental destruction accompanying the so-called opening of the West and did everything he could to preserve precious forests. As a young man, he had tremendous respect for Emerson, who made a special effort to visit him in Yosemite Valley.

Emerson was sixty-eight, Muir thirty-three. The meeting occurred in May 1871, two years after the First Transcontinental Railroad (known then as the Pacific Railroad) began operation. It was a moving experience for Muir, who described Emerson as the "most serene, majestic, sequoia-like soul I ever met. His smile was as sweet and calm as morning light on mountains."[2]

Muir continued the struggle to protect the natural world right up to his death. Emerson wrote, "In the woods, we return to reason and faith."[3] Muir kept Emerson in his heart throughout his life.

MADE BETTER IN NATURE

BOSCO: There are many expressions in writings by Emerson, Thoreau, and Whitman to the effect that, in her fullness and organic balance, nature is a sacred site. So that when nature is diminished in any way, some part of humankind's divinity is proportionally diminished.

IKEDA: Makiguchi wrote:

> As children we grow up in the shadows of the mountains and come to love them almost as we love our parents. Their presence grows within our minds and deeply affects our lives and personalities, unconsciously.[4]

He further asserted that the vast European world of nature was a formative influence for great educators like Johann H. Pestalozzi in Switzerland and Johann Friedrich Herbart in Germany. The natural world has the power to evoke and cultivate the limitless possibilities inherent in human beings. As a geographer, Makiguchi was aware of this from an early stage.

I understand that Thoreau was an excellent botanist and geologist.

MYERSON: In the January 7, 1857, entry in his journal, Thoreau wrote:

> There is nothing so sanative, so poetic, as a walk in the woods and fields even now, when I meet none abroad for pleasure. Nothing so inspires me and excites such serene and profitable thought. The objects are elevating.[5]

BOSCO: Thoreau interacted with and interpreted nature as a place of refuge, as a site of healing and health, and as a moral environment in which, by immersing himself, he may be made better.

As I shared earlier (see Conversation Twelve), he conveyed this in a journal entry for August 23, 1853:

> Live in each season as it passes; breathe the air, drink the drink, taste the fruit, and resign yourself to the influences of each. Let them be your only diet drink and botanical medicines. In August live on berries. . . . Grow green with spring, yellow and ripe with autumn. Drink of each season's influence as a vial, a true panacea of all remedies mixed for your especial use.[6]

THE "SOUL OF THE WHOLE"

IKEDA: The following examples indicate how strongly Eastern philosophy influenced the way Emerson, Thoreau, and other philosophers of the American Renaissance viewed nature.

In his essay "The Over-Soul," Emerson wrote:

> Meantime within man is the soul of the whole; the wise silence; the universal beauty, to which every part and particle is equally related; the eternal ONE. . . . We see the world piece by piece, as the sun, the moon, the animal, the tree; but the whole, of which these are the shining parts, is the soul.[7]

In *Walden*, Thoreau wrote, "In the morning I bathe my intellect in the stupendous and cosmogonal philosophy of the Bhagvat Geeta."[8]

BOSCO: In his notes to his edition of his father's *Works* (1903–04), Edward Waldo Emerson quoted a visitor to Concord from Calcutta shortly after Emerson's death:

Amidst this ceaseless, sleepless din and clash of Western Materialism, this heat of restless energy, the character of Emerson shines
upon India serene as the evening star. He seems to some of us to
have been a geographical mistake.[9]

This suggests the extent to which Emerson and Thoreau's
thought transcended the boundaries between East and West.

MYERSON: Emerson's notebook titled "Orientalist," edited by Dr.
Bosco, reveals the extent to which Eastern philosophy and religion
influenced him.[10]

BOSCO: The range of the notebook is unusual because Emerson
recorded in it both the thoughts he had while studying Eastern culture and his translations of a substantial amount of Persian poetry
from German sources. From the Persian poets, Emerson learned
imaginative freedom, occasional primitivism, and the comprehen-
sive unity of Brahman faith. Translating their poems reinforced
Emerson's wonder at nature's prospect and provided him with relief from the crassness, brutality, and vulgarity he encountered in
nineteenth-century materialistic culture.

IKEDA: The love Emerson and Thoreau felt for nature seems essentially different from prevailing attitudes today. They did not
believe nature existed only for human use. Their love of nature
brimmed with gratitude and the irrepressible desire for human
beings, as part of nature, to improve themselves through enjoying
it, observing it, being astonished by it, and connecting with its
divinity.

ONENESS WITH NATURE

BOSCO: As you suggest, President Ikeda, the difference between
Thoreau's approach to nature and that of people today mirrors a

fundamental difference in the values he advocated while living in nature and those that many exercise today. It suggests, too, that the great distinction Thoreau earned as a lover of nature was a function of the purity and simplicity of his character. He opened himself completely to nature and yielded himself to her influences on his mind, senses, and heart.

MYERSON: Thoreau immersed himself in the natural world both physically and philosophically. While Emerson suggested nature might be an "apocalypse of the mind,"[11] meaning something that was created by the observer, Thoreau believed in the physicality of nature: The world exists, and it is up to us to read its lessons correctly. Moreover, nature is not separate from us: We are part of it.

IKEDA: The opening passage of "Solitude," in *Walden*, vividly portrays Thoreau's own experience of oneness with nature:

> This is a delicious evening, when the whole body is one sense, and imbibes delight through every pore. I go and come with a strange liberty in Nature, a part of herself.[12]

We can almost hear the trees rustling in the wind as Thoreau relates, breathlessly, his feeling for nature.

BOSCO: Nature provided Thoreau with irrefutable evidence both of its divinity and of his own. Writing in his journal on January 23, 1858, he observed:

> To insure health, a man's relation to Nature must come very near to a personal one; he must be conscious of a friendliness in her. . . . I cannot conceive of any life worthy of the name that lacks a certain tender relation to Nature. This it is which makes winter warm, and supplies society in the desert and wilderness. Unless Nature sympathizes with and speaks to us, as it were, the most fertile and blooming regions are barren and dreary.[13]

MYERSON: Later in the "Solitude" chapter of *Walden*, Thoreau wrote:

> In the midst of a gentle rain . . . I was suddenly sensible of such sweet and beneficent society in Nature, . . . as made the fancied advantages of human neighborhood insignificant, and I have never thought of them since.[14]

In this passage, he is saying that the conveniences of civilized society are insignificant in comparison to the friendship of nature.

IKEDA: Thoreau's words convey the sense of being immersed in and conversing with nature. They express the joy of communication between the mind and nature.

As Thoreau said, nature supports human life and offers a place of healing and nurturing. In the pursuit of utilitarian aims, however, modern society has exploited and damaged it. Such egocentric behavior not only disrupts the harmony of humanity and nature but also severs relations among human beings, breeding destructive attitudes.

BOSCO: Nature was Thoreau's "herb" guaranteeing his physical and mental well-being. While immersed in nature, he transcended the limitations of nationalism and his specific locale to become a global citizen.

IKEDA: Dr. Bosco, you mentioned that nature provided Thoreau with evidence of its divinity and of his own. For Thoreau, divinity seems to have been existence—the fundamental current flowing through nature and the universe.

It is both outside the self and within the self. It can thus be called the truth permeating all nature, the cosmos, and humanity.

Buddhism teaches that the supremely noble entity called the Buddha nature shines in all things. It seems to me that this Buddha nature and what Emerson and Thoreau refer to as divinity are the same ultimate entity or truth within the cosmos and human life.

Furthermore, these ideas point in the same direction: toward discovering and experiencing truth through interacting with the environment. A primary qualification for a global citizen, as Dr. Bosco suggests, is to manifest this truth within oneself and transcend one's limitations, thus contributing to the good of all humankind.

CONVERSATION EIGHTEEN

"Our Prospects Brighten"

The Value of Practical Experience

IKEDA: Can we next discuss prospects for making the twenty-first century a century devoted to the environment, human rights, and life? The United Nations Decade of Education for Sustainable Development started in 2005. Various countries and nongovernmental organizations like the SGI are cooperating to make the project a success.

For example, the SGI sponsored an exhibition on the environment titled "Seeds of Change," which has already toured more than twenty countries. A film titled *A Quiet Revolution*, which the SGI produced with the Earth Charter Initiative, was screened at the World Summit on Sustainable Development in South Africa (August 2002) and has attracted great interest from many parts of the world.

MYERSON: These are all significant undertakings. Education is of the greatest importance in building a new age.

Young people must realize that they can do something to change things. Environmental education early in life will accustom them to conscientious courses of action like recycling resources and protecting the natural environment.

IKEDA: The first step in environmental education is sincere observation of the lives of others and the nature that surrounds us. Makiguchi believed such observation of our own communities is the starting point to expand our view to include the whole world. Thus, the "geography of human life," as he called it.

MYERSON: His ideas and proposals remain important in our search for the optimum environmental education.

IKEDA: In a sense, Thoreau's days at Walden Pond were spent in observation of his native district.

BOSCO: Thoreau included observations of his native district in his journal. For instance, he wrote in August 1851, "Holidays are prepared for me, and my path is strewn with flowers."[1] And, again, in December of 1856, "I have never got over my surprise that I should have been born into the most estimable place in all the world, and in the very nick of time, too."[2]

Thoreau paid tribute to Concord both as his muse and the site in which he fashioned his life of radical individualism. The lesson his life imparts is that we all must find our own Concords, our own Waldens.

IKEDA: People who have found their own Concords and Waldens, while keeping their feet firmly planted on the ground, can embrace the whole world.

BOSCO: To students who ask whether Thoreau was a philosopher, I say "Yes." From my point of view, Thoreau was a true philosopher to the extent that he broke with the traditional but too often negative image of philosophers who speculate rather than act. Speculation without action had no meaning for Thoreau, as he revealed in his critique of traditional philosophers in this passage from the first chapter of *Walden*:

> There are nowadays professors of philosophy, but not philosophers. Yet it is admirable to profess because it was once admirable to live. To be a philosopher is not merely to have subtle thoughts, nor even to found a school, but so to love wisdom as to live according to its dictates a life of simplicity, independence, magnanimity, and trust. It is to solve some of the problems of life, not only theoretically, but practically.[3]

As a theory, this sounds very Emersonian. It is also very American.

For me, this aspect of Thoreau's belief makes him a philosopher of pragmatism, the philosophic system that Dewey, William James, and others of a later generation of Americans would formalize as a genuinely and distinctively original national philosophy.

IKEDA: Makiguchi considered practical experience the core of his educational system. He felt a strong affinity with Dewey, to whose works he frequently alluded. Buddhism, too, insists that theory becomes convincing only when verified by experience.

BOSCO: I regard Thoreau not only as a "professor" of nature and advocate for the preservation of the environment but also as a political philosopher. He has exerted both a philosophical *and* a political influence on succeeding generations through those philosophic doctrines Dr. Myerson summarized as "simplicity, independence, magnanimity, and trust."

IKEDA: His clarion call against authoritarianism transcended ethnic and national boundaries to move the minds of the masses everywhere and influence history itself. As we have already pointed out, Thoreau's philosophy enlightened and profoundly inspired a range of popular movements for human dignity and liberty.

Thoreau's Political Legacy

MYERSON: In 1931, Gandhi told a reporter:

> Why, of course I read Thoreau. I read *Walden* first in . . . 1906
> and his ideas influenced me greatly. I adopted some of them and
> recommended the study of Thoreau to all my friends who were
> helping me in the cause of Indian independence. Why, I actually
> took the name of my movement from Thoreau's essay, "On the
> Duty of Civil Disobedience."[4]

Gandhi wrote President Franklin Roosevelt in 1942 that he had "profited greatly by the writings of Thoreau and Emerson."[5]

Martin Luther King Jr., too, was influenced by reading "Civil Disobedience" during a formative period in his life. As a college student in 1956, he was beginning the Montgomery, Alabama, bus boycotts that would galvanize the civil rights movement.

Of that time, he recalled:

> I had been moved when I first read this work. I became convinced
> that what we were prepared to do in Montgomery was related to
> what Thoreau had expressed. We were simply saying to the white
> community, "We can no longer lend our cooperation to an evil
> system."[6]

King described the essay as his "first intellectual contact with the theory of nonviolent resistance."[7] Writing in 1962, he commented that "Civil Disobedience" convinced him that "non-cooperation with evil is as much a moral obligation as is cooperation with good."[8]

IKEDA: During the bus boycott movement, ordinary citizens threw down the gauntlet by saying "No" to social injustice. I have enjoyed conversations both in Los Angeles and Tokyo with Rosa Parks, who was arrested for refusing to move to the rear of the bus (on Dec. 1, 1955).

She remembered that the more that black people gave in to white people, the worse white people treated them. Indeed, leaving evil uncorrected only aggravates it. Champions of civil rights like King and Parks courageously challenged immense social evil.

BOSCO: The Thoreau Society owns an audiotape of King speaking of the centrality of Thoreau's doctrine of nonviolent protest to his own participation in the civil rights movement. Although the pent-up frustration of the black community in America during the mid-twentieth century might have justified violence to end white oppression, King chose peaceful protest as the best means to change people's minds and hearts.

IKEDA: Consistent, unwavering nonviolence demands real courage. As Gandhi said:

> It would be wholly wrong . . . to say that non-violence is a weapon of the weak. The use of non-violence requires greater bravery than that of violence.[9]

BOSCO: For both Gandhi and King, "Civil Disobedience" served as a handbook for theorizing and enacting a political philosophy of nonviolent protest. On the audiotape I mentioned, King explicitly comments on the importance of this text both to him as a statement of philosophy and to his people as a statement of political philosophy, unexpectedly emphasizing nonviolence in connection with civil protest.

IKEDA: My friend M. S. Swaminathan, the father of the Green Revolution, insists that nonviolence education is the most important aspect of environmental education. Nonviolence is essential for symbiosis among human beings and between humanity and nature. In addition to courage, nonviolence requires love and compassion toward others, humble respect for diversity, and unrelenting self-control—all the traits human beings need in working with nature and the environment.

MYERSON: What you say reminds me of an interview with Arun Gandhi published in the *SGI Quarterly*. Arun Gandhi is Gandhi's grandchild and a member of the Thoreau Society. In the interview, he said:

> For Gandhi . . . nonviolence was not merely the passive acceptance of the violence of others but a transformative philosophy and practice that went to the very root of our understanding of ourselves and our relationships with others and with the world. . . .[10]

IKEDA: To make the twenty-first century a century devoted to the environment and human rights, the SGI is conducting its activities worldwide. Our axial philosophy, again, is human revolution: the idea that an improved society and peace for the world starts with self-reformation.

The industrial and technological revolutions could be called external revolutions. Much of the progress they set in motion, however, has already reached an impasse.

The arrogant egoism that spawned our notion of conquering nature has resulted in a threat to humanity itself. We must overcome our present crises by attending to a fundamental revolution within the human being: the human revolution.

Aware of this, we of the SGI are conducting a humanistic movement, the core of which is strengthening peace, culture, and education. On the occasion of the World Summit on Sustainable Development in South Africa, I issued an environmental proposal titled "The Challenge of Global Empowerment: Education for a Sustainable Future."[11] I argued that environmental problems cannot be resolved without overcoming human egoism.

SAVING NATURE, SAVING OURSELVES

MYERSON: The SGI's concept of a human revolution emphasizing the importance of human rights and the environment is an excellent way to encourage both environmental and personal reform.

Too often movements that stress personal development and organizations that promote the conservation of the environment fail to connect the two.

BOSCO: Thoreau thought of his morning bath in Walden Pond as a religious activity. To plunge oneself into the world of nature makes individual rebirth possible. He believed that the connectedness of humanity and nature means that by saving nature, we save ourselves.

MYERSON: It is essential to maintain this balance between action directed toward the outside world and refinement of our interior world. The service-learning movement in contemporary American education parallels SGI ideas. In service-learning courses, students combine book learning with community service; for example, reading about the natural world and then volunteering to help at the zoo or clean up a city park.

BOSCO: For individuals and nations as well, environmental education must cultivate an eye for self-observation. Some people think the developing nations must learn from industrialized nations, which supposedly have the know-how to cope with environmental problems.

But this is a mistake because it is the unbridled industrialization and misuse of natural resources on the part of the so-called developed nations that have brought on environmental destruction. Few industrialized nations display the political will or the economic intention of sacrificing their national desires and economic interests for the preservation of natural resources. This is why we must seek models among primitive cultures with a deep affinity for and sense of unity with the land as a heaven-sent blessing.

IKEDA: Thoreau was an early advocate of human rights and environmental conservation, which have become twenty-first-century watchwords. His pioneering work in these areas deserves the highest praise.

He raised and took as his philosophical point of departure the questions of what is most important for humanity and how human beings should improve themselves. In this respect, succeeding generations have striven to catch up with him.

Instead of fading away, his philosophy has become increasingly important. I imagine this explains the Thoreau Society's raison d'être.

BOSCO: Yes, it does, President Ikeda; it explains the mission of the Thoreau Society.

ANOTHER STEP

BOSCO: If you will permit us, since Dr. Myerson and I have given much thought to how to summarize our discussions with you, we would appreciate the opportunity to speak here in one voice.

Your kind invitation to us to engage in these conversations has provided us with occasions to put into practice both Emerson and Thoreau's devotion to the art, Emerson said, of conversation or—to use a term that seems more appropriate here and reflects an SGI ideal that you have devoted your life to promoting—dialogue.

It is in exchanges such as these that people truly meet. Here, people share ideas and ideals, and by listening to the words and considering the thoughts of others, they appreciate that there are many valid ways of understanding their place in this world.

To have shared our ideas about Emerson, Thoreau, and Whitman, and their relevance today as promoters of ideals that have been reenacted in the wisdom of Makiguchi and Toda, as well as in that of Gandhi and King, and to have witnessed those ideals put into practice at both Soka University of Japan and the Soka University of America has been an honor, indeed.

IKEDA: The honor is mine. I was enlightened by your great intellect and philosophy.

BOSCO: In his wonderful essay on "The Poet"—from which you, President Ikeda, have quoted on several occasions—Emerson wrote, "Words are . . . actions, and actions are a kind of words."[12] For Dr. Myerson and me, the most important legacy of our conversations will be the actions that follow from the ideas on individualism, community, the environment, and the like that we have shared together.

In fact, as you so well know, our words have already been put into action in the Ikeda Forum, which you have inaugurated and generously supported at the Boston Research Center for the 21st Century (renamed the Ikeda Center for Peace, Learning, and Dialogue in 2009). During our first Ikeda Forum, in 2004, we took up the challenge that Thoreau issues in *Walden* to create our own Waldens in each and every generation. This year (2005), in what by all participants' accounts was a simply masterful discussion of Whitman's poetry and place in the international community, the ideas and ideals we have spoken about in our conversations have been given expression in action.

So, President Ikeda, we thank you not only for your kind and thoughtful words throughout our conversations but also for the inspiring way in which you have succeeded in putting those words into action.

IKEDA: The following passage is from "Spring," the final chapter of *Walden*:

> As every season seems best to us in its turn, so the coming of spring is like the creation of Cosmos out of Chaos and the realization of the Golden Age. . . . A single gentle rain makes the grass many shades greener. So our prospects brighten on the influx of better thoughts.[13]

I see in Thoreau's mighty hope and confidence a great spiritual source for the American Renaissance. Before we can build a new age, perhaps we must first plumb the depths of chaos.

Our most urgent task is to usher in the springtime of a new age of peace while continuing to learn from the humanistic spirit of Emerson and Thoreau. I sincerely hope that our conversations represent another step along the great road of hope for human history. Please allow me to express my sincere thanks to you, Dr. Bosco and Dr. Myerson, for staying the long course in our fascinating discussions.

Notes

FOREWORD

1. See *Todai* (*Lighthouse*), nos. 527–44 (August 2004–January 2006), and *Utsukushiki seimei—chikyu to ikiru* (Renaissance of Life, Light of Poetic Heart) (Tokyo: Mainichi Shimbun, 2006).
2. Walt Whitman, *Leaves of Grass*, in *Poetry and Prose*, ed. Justin Kaplan (New York: Library of America, 1982), p. 188.
3. *The Journal of Henry D. Thoreau*, ed. Bradford Torrey (Boston: Houghton, Mifflin and Company, 1906), 8:88.
4. Emerson to Carlyle, June 30, 1840, in *The Correspondence of Emerson and Carlyle*, ed. Joseph Slater (New York and London: Columbia University Press, 1964), p. 272.
5. *The Journals and Miscellaneous Notebooks of Ralph Waldo Emerson*, eds. William H. Gilman, Ralph H. Orth, et al. (Cambridge, MA, and London: Harvard University Press, 1960–1982), 7:342.
6. Ralph Waldo Emerson, *Representative Men*, in *Essays and Lectures*, ed. Joel Porte (New York: Library of America, 1983), p. 621.
7. Whitman, *Leaves of Grass*, in *Poetry and Prose*, p. 242.
8. Daisaku Ikeda, "Poetry," excerpted from "Poetry—A View of Humankind," *Symphonic Poems with Nature* (Tokyo: Seikyo Press, 2002), p. 8.
9. *The Journal of Henry D. Thoreau*, 5:34–35.

Conversation One

1. *The Journal of Henry D. Thoreau*, 5:35.
2. Ibid., 5:135.
3. Emerson, "Thoreau," in *Essays and Poems*, eds. Joel Porte, Harold Bloom, and Paul Kane (New York: Library of America College Editions, 1983), p. 1024.

Conversation Two

1. Daisaku Ikeda, *A New Humanism: The University Addresses of Daisaku Ikeda* (New York and Tokyo: Weatherhill, Inc., 1996), p. 204.
2. Ibid.
3. *The Writings of Nichiren Daishonin*, vol. I (Tokyo: Soka Gakkai, 1999), p. 457.

Conversation Three

1. J. Hector St. John de Crévecoeur, *Letters from an American Farmer and Sketches of Eighteenth-Century America* (New York: Penguin Books, 1981), p. 70.
2. Emerson, "The American Scholar," in *Essays and Lectures*, p. 53.
3. Emerson, *Nature*, in *Essays and Lectures*, p. 48.
4. Ibid., p. 7.
5. Soka Gakkai International official website, <http://www.sgi.org/charter.html>.

Conversation Four

1. Henry David Thoreau, *A Week on the Concord and Merrimack Rivers*, in *A Week, Walden, The Maine Woods, Cape Cod*, ed. Robert F. Sayre (New York: Library of America, 1985), p. 7.
2. *The Journal of Henry D. Thoreau*, 9:160.
3. *Mahatma: Life of Gandhi 1869–1948*, video by Vithalbhai Jhaveri (The Gandhi National Memorial Fund in cooperation with the Films Division of the Government of India, 1968), Reel 31.

4. Emerson, "Thoreau," in *Essays and Poems*, p. 1009.
5. Thoreau, *Walden*, in *A Week, Walden, The Maine Woods, Cape Cod*, p. 393.
6. Henry David Thoreau, *Collected Essays and Poems*, ed. Elizabeth Hall Witherell (New York: Library of America, 2001), p. 552.
7. Ibid., p. 338.
8. Emerson to Carlyle, May 30, 1841, in *The Correspondence of Emerson and Carlyle*, p. 300.
9. Ralph Waldo Emerson, "Concord Walks," in *The Complete Works of Ralph Waldo Emerson*, vol. XII (New York: Houghton, Mifflin and Company, 1903–04), p. 176.
10. Ralph Waldo Emerson, "Poetry and the Imagination," in vol. VIII—Letters and Social Aims, at "The Works of Ralph Waldo Emerson," < http://www.rwe.org/ >.

CONVERSATION FIVE

1. Thoreau, *Walden*, in *A Week, Walden, The Maine Woods, Cape Cod*, p. 325.
2. Ibid., p. 394.
3. Ibid., p. 496.
4. *The Writings of Nichiren Daishonin*, vol. I, p. 997.
5. Thoreau, *Walden*, in *A Week, Walden, The Maine Woods, Cape Cod*, p. 471.
6. Ibid., p. 329.
7. Ibid., p. 580.
8. *The Journal of Henry D. Thoreau*, 7:88.
9. Emerson, *Nature*, in *Essays and Lectures*, p. 48.
10. *The Journal of Henry D. Thoreau*, 14:277.
11. *The Correspondence of Henry David Thoreau*, eds. Walter Harding and Carl Bode (Washington Square: New York University Press, 1958), p. 217.
12. *The Book of Kindred Sayings (Samyutta Nikaya)*, ed. and trans. F. L. Woodward, 5 vols. (London: The Pali Text Society, 1922), 1:2
13. *The Journal of Henry D. Thoreau*, 1:295.
14. Ibid., 9:146.
15. Ibid., 9:337.
16. Ibid., 3:165.

17. Thoreau, "A Plea for Captain John Brown," in *Collected Essays and Poems*, p. 397.

18. Ibid., p. 410.

19. Emerson, "Thoreau," in *Essays and Poems*, p. 1024.

20. Thoreau, *Walden*, in *A Week, Walden, The Maine Woods, Cape Cod*, p. 347.

21. *The Journal of Henry D. Thoreau*, 8:200–21.

22. Ibid., 8:221–22.

Conversation Six

1. *The Journal of Henry D. Thoreau*, 2:101.

2. Emerson, "Address at Opening of Concord Free Public Library," in Volume XI—Miscellanies, at "The Works of Ralph Waldo Emerson," <http://www.rwe.org/>.

3. Thoreau, *Walden*, in *A Week, Walden, The Maine Woods, Cape Cod*, p. 405.

4. Ibid., p. 404.

5. *The Correspondence of Henry David Thoreau*, p. 249.

6. Ibid., p. 545.

7. *The Later Lectures of Ralph Waldo Emerson, 1843–1871*, ed. Ronald A. Bosco and Joel Myerson, 2 vols. (Athens, GA: University of Georgia Press, 2001), 2:230.

8. Thoreau, *Walden*, in *A Week, Walden, The Maine Woods, Cape Cod*, p. 403.

9. Ibid.

10. Ibid., p. 408.

11. *The Journal of Henry D. Thoreau*, 2:192.

12. Henry David Thoreau, *Walden*, in *A Week, Walden, The Maine Woods, Cape Cod*, p. 405.

13. Ibid., p. 403.

14. Ralph Waldo Emerson, "Books," in Volume VII—Society and Solitude, at "The Works of Ralph Waldo Emerson," <http://www.rwe.org/>.

15. Victor Hugo, "Victor Hugo on the Liberty of the Press," in *The Public School Speaker and Reader*, ed. J. E. Carpenter (London: Frederick Warne and Company, 1869), p. 252.

Conversation Seven

1. Thoreau, *Walden*, in *A Week, Walden, The Maine Woods, Cape Cod*, pp. 469–70.
2. *The Journal of Henry D. Thoreau*, 5:135.
3. Thoreau, *Walden*, in *A Week, Walden, The Maine Woods, Cape Cod*, p. 513.
4. Ibid., p. 394.
5. Ibid., p. 378.
6. Ibid., p. 559.
7. Thoreau, "Civil Disobedience," in *Collected Essays and Poems*, p. 224.
8. Thoreau, *Walden*, in *A Week, Walden, The Maine Woods, Cape Cod*, p. 459.
9. *The Writings of Nichiren Daishonin*, vol. I, p. 579.
10. *The Journal of Henry D. Thoreau*, 2:404.
11. Ibid., 8:88.
12. Thoreau, "Civil Disobedience," in *Collected Essays and Poems*, p. 213.
13. Daisaku Ikeda, *The Human Revolution*, book 1 (Santa Monica, CA: World Tribune Press, 2004), p. viii.
14. Thoreau, "Civil Disobedience," in *Collected Essays and Poems*, p. 213.
15. Thoreau, *Walden*, in *A Week, Walden, The Maine Woods, Cape Cod*, p. 329.
16. Thoreau, "Civil Disobedience," in *Collected Essays and Poems*, p. 209.

Conversation Eight

1. *Emerson in His Journals*, ed. Joel Porte (Cambridge, MA, and London: The Belknap Press of Harvard University Press, 1982), pp. 247–48. The definitive edition of Emerson's journals, from which Porte drew but regularized the selections included in his volume, is *The Journals and Miscellaneous Notebooks of Ralph Waldo Emerson*, eds. William H. Gilman, Ralph H. Orth, et al., 16 vols. (Cambridge, MA, and London: Harvard University Press, 1960–1982).
2. Edward Waldo Emerson, *Emerson in Concord* (Boston: Houghton, Mifflin and Company, 1890), p. 21.
3. *The Journals and Miscellaneous Notebooks of Ralph Waldo Emerson*, 7:342.

4. *Emerson in His Journals*, p. 81.

5. Emerson, "The 'Lord's Supper' Sermon," in *Essays and Poems*, pp. 964–65.

6. Daisaku Ikeda, *A New Humanism*, p. 157.

7. *Emerson in His Journals*, p. 83.

8. Ronald A. Bosco and Joel Myerson, *The Emerson Brothers: A Fraternal Biography in Letters* (Oxford and New York: Oxford University Press, 2006), pp. 66–67.

CONVERSATION NINE

1. Emerson, "Compensation," in *Essays and Lectures*, p. 302.

2. Daisaku Ikeda, *Learning from the Gosho: The Eternal Teachings of Nichiren Daishonin* (Santa Monica, CA: World Tribune Press, 1997), p. 170.

3. *The Journals and Miscellaneous Notebooks of Ralph Waldo Emerson*, 4:252.

4. *Selected Writings of Ralph Waldo Emerson*, ed. William H. Gillman (New York: Signet Classics, 2003), pp. 155–56.

5. Emerson, "The Poet," in *Essays and Lectures*, p. 465.

6. Ibid.

7. Whitman, *Leaves of Grass*, in *Poetry and Prose*, p. 188.

8. Emerson, "Terminus," in *Essays and Poems*, p. 1242.

9. Emerson, *Representative Men*, in *Essays and Lectures*, p. 641.

CONVERSATION TEN

1. Emerson, *Nature*, in *Essays and Lectures*, p. 47.

2. Ibid., p. 7.

3. Emerson, "Compensation," in *Essays and Lectures*, p. 302.

4. *The Journals and Miscellaneous Notebooks of Ralph Waldo Emerson*, 7:202–03.

5. Emerson, *Nature*, in *Essays and Lectures*, p. 7.

6. Ibid., p. 11.

7. *Emerson in His Journals*, p. 111.

8. Emerson, *Nature*, in *Essays and Lectures*, p. 47.

9. Ibid., p. 48.

10. Emerson, "The American Scholar," in *Essays and Lectures*, p. 53.

11. Ibid., p. 56.

12. Ibid., p. 57.

13. Ibid.

14. Ibid., p. 60.

15. Emerson, "The Divinity School Address," in *Essays and Lectures*, p. 87.

16. Ibid., p. 89.

17. Ibid., p. 91.

18. *Emerson in His Journals*, p. 86.

19. Emerson, "The Divinity School Address," in *Essays and Lectures*, pp. 88–89.

20. Andrews Norton, "A Discourse on the Latest Form of Infidelity" (1839), at the History Tools website, <http://www.historytools.org/sources/norton.html>.

Conversation Eleven

1. Emerson, "Self-Reliance," in *Essays and Lectures*, p. 265.

2. Daisaku Ikeda, "The Humanism of the Middle Way—Dawn of a Global Civilization," 2002 peace proposal, <http://www.sgi-usa.org/newsandevents/doc/peace2002.pdf>.

3. Emerson, "The Poet," in *Essays and Lectures*, p. 448.

4. *Emerson in His Journals*, p. 407.

5. *The Journals and Miscellaneous Notebooks of Ralph Waldo Emerson*, 4:353–54.

6. Ibid.

7. Emerson, "The Method of Nature," in *Essays and Lectures*, p. 122.

8. Ibid.

9. Emerson, "The Divinity School Address," in *Essays and Lectures*, pp. 76 and 88.

10. Emerson, *Representative Men*, in *Essays and Lectures*, p. 728.

11. Ibid., p. 631.

12. *Emerson in His Journals*, p. 236.

13. Ibid.

CONVERSATION TWELVE

1. Thoreau, *Walden*, in *A Week, Walden, The Maine Woods, Cape Cod*, p. 326.
2. Ibid., p. 329.
3. Ibid., p. 358.
4. Ibid., p. 434.
5. Ibid., p. 577.
6. Ibid., p. 495.
7. Ibid., p. 352.
8. Ibid., p. 363.
9. *The Journal of Henry D. Thoreau*, 8:44.
10. Ibid., 5:394.
11. Nichiren, *The Record of the Orally Transmitted Teachings*, trans. Burton Watson (Tokyo: Soka Gakkai, 2004), p. 11.
12. Ralph Waldo Emerson, "The Rule of Life," in *Selected Lectures of Ralph Waldo Emerson*, eds. Ronald A. Bosco and Joel Myerson (Athens, GA, and London: University of Georgia Press, 2005), pp. 348–60.
13. Thoreau, *Walden*, in *A Week, Walden, The Maine Woods, Cape Cod*, p. 578.

CONVERSATION THIRTEEN

1. *The Journals of Bronson Alcott*, ed. Odell Shepard (Boston: Little, Brown and Company, 1938), p. 289.
2. *The Correspondence of Henry David Thoreau*, p. 441.
3. *The Journals of Bronson Alcott*, pp. 290–91.
4. *The Correspondence of Henry David Thoreau*, p. 441.
5. Ibid., p. 445.
6. Ibid.
7. Whitman, *Leaves of Grass*, in *Poetry and Prose*, p. 207.
8. *The Correspondence of Henry David Thoreau*, p. 445.
9. *The Writings of Nichiren Daishonin*, vol. II (Tokyo: Soka Gakkai, 2006), p. 843.
10. Ibid., p. 844.
11. Whitman, *Leaves of Grass*, in *Poetry and Prose*, p. 210.
12. Ibid., p. 246.

13. Emerson, "Self Reliance," in *Essays and Lectures*, p. 265.
14. Emerson, "The Poet," in *Essays and Lectures*, p. 465.
15. Ibid., p. 456.
16. Ibid., pp. 456–57.
17. *The Writings of Nichiren Daishonin*, vol. I, p. 421.
18. Emerson, "The Poet," in *Essays and Lectures*, p. 457.
19. *The Correspondence of Henry David Thoreau*, p. 445.
20. Emerson, "The Poet," in *Essays and Lectures*, p. 465.

Conversation Fourteen

1. Daisaku Ikeda official website, <http://www.daisakuikeda.org/index. php?id=352>.
2. Emerson, "Education," in Volume X—Lectures and Biographical Sketches, at "The Works of Ralph Waldo Emerson," <http://www. rwe.org/>.
3. *Emerson in His Journals*, p. 128.
4. *The Selected Lectures of Ralph Waldo Emerson*, p. xxvi.
5. Francis Greenwood Peabody, "The Germ of the Graduate School," *The Harvard Graduates' Magazine* 27 (1918), pp. 180–81.
6. Tsunesaburo Makiguchi, *Soka Kyoiku Taikei (The System of Value-Creating Pedagogy)*, vol. IV (Tokyo: Seikyo Shimbun, 1980), p. 30.
7. Emerson, "The Divinity School Address," in *Essays and Lectures*, p. 85.
8. John Dewey, *The Essential Dewey, Volume 1: Pragmatism, Education, Democracy*, eds. Larry A. Hickman and Thomas M. Alexander (Bloomington, IN: Indiana University Press, 1998), p. 238.
9. Tsunesaburo Makiguchi, *Education for Creative Living: Ideas and Proposals of Tsunesaburo Makiguchi*, trans. Alfred Birnbaum, ed. Dayle M. Bethel (Ames, IA: Iowa State University Press, 1989), p. 168.
10. Makiguchi, *Education for Creative Living* p. 25.

Conversation Fifteen

1. Thoreau, *Walden*, in *A Week, Walden, The Maine Woods, Cape Cod*, p. 409.

2. Walter Harding, *The Days of Henry Thoreau* (New York: Knopf, 1965), p. 51.
3. Thoreau, *Walden*, in *A Week, Walden, The Maine Woods, Cape Cod*, p. 409.
4. Rose Hawthorne Lathrop, *Memories of Hawthorne* (Cambridge, MA: The Riverside Press, 1897), p. 92.
5. Daisaku Ikeda, "Poetry," *Symphonic Poems with Nature*, p. 8.
6. *The Journal of Henry D. Thoreau*, 9:208.
7. Dewey, *The Essential Dewey*, pp. 236–37.
8. Daisaku Ikeda, *Soka Education: A Buddhist Vision for Teachers, Students and Parents* (Santa Monica, CA: Middleway Press, 2001), p. 70.
9. Thoreau, *Walden*, in *A Week, Walden, The Maine Woods, Cape Cod*, p. 394.
10. Ibid.

CONVERSATION SIXTEEN

1. Kunikida Doppo, *Musashino*, in *River Mist and Other Stories*, trans. David Chibbett (Tokyo, New York and San Francisco: Kodansha International Ltd., 1982), p. 106.
2. Thoreau, *Walden*, in *A Week, Walden, The Maine Woods, Cape Cod*, p. 459.
3. *The Journal of Henry D. Thoreau*, 2:472.
4. Ibid., 1:296.
5. Ibid., 2:392.
6. Ibid., 2:413.
7. Ibid., 2:416.
8. *The Writings of Nichiren Daishonin*, vol. I, p. 1000.

CONVERSATION SEVENTEEN

1. Daisaku Ikeda, *For the Leaders of the 21st Century: Founder's Memorable Remarks* (Aliso Viejo, CA: Soka Student Government Association, 2005), p. 15.
2. *John of the Mountains: The Unpublished Journals of John Muir* (Madison, WI: University of Madison Press, 1979), p. 436.

3. Emerson, *Nature*, in *Essays and Lectures*, p. 10.
4. Tsunesaburo Makiguchi, *A Geography of Human Life* (San Francisco, CA: Caddo Gap Press, 2002), p. 62.
5. *The Journal of Henry D. Thoreau*, 9:208.
6. Ibid., 5:394.
7. Emerson, "The Over-Soul," in *Essays and Lectures*, p. 386.
8. Thoreau, *Walden*, in *A Week, Walden, The Maine Woods, Cape Cod*, p. 559.
9. *The Complete Works of Ralph Waldo Emerson*, volume VIII, ed. Edward Waldo Emerson (Boston and New York: Houghton, Mifflin and Company, 1903–04), p. 413.
10. *The Topical Notebooks of Ralph Waldo Emerson*, vol. 2, ed. Ronald A. Bosco (Columbia, MO: University of Missouri Press, 1993), pp. 37–141.
11. Emerson, *Nature*, in *Essays and Lectures*, p. 32.
12. Thoreau, *Walden*, in *A Week, Walden, The Maine Woods, Cape Cod*, p. 425.
13. *The Journal of Henry D. Thoreau*, 10:252.
14. Thoreau, *Walden*, in *A Week, Walden, The Maine Woods, Cape Cod*, p. 427.

CONVERSATION EIGHTEEN

1. *The Journal of Henry D. Thoreau*, 2:392.
2. Ibid., 9:160.
3. Thoreau, *Walden*, in *A Week, Walden, The Maine Woods, Cape Cod*, p. 334.
4. Yogesh Chadha, *Gandhi: A Life* (Hoboken: John Wiley & Sons, 1997), p. 138.
5. *The Gandhi Reader: A Sourcebook of His Life and Writings*, ed. Homer A. Jack (New York: Grove/Atlantic, 1994), p. 357.
6. Martin Luther King Jr., *Stride Toward Freedom* (San Francisco: Harper & Row, 1958), p. 51.
7. Ibid., p. 91.
8. *Black & White in American Culture: An Anthology from the Massachusetts Review*, eds. Jules Chametzky and Sidney Kaplan (Amherst, MA: University of Massachusetts Press, 1969), p. 105.

9. *The Gandhi Reader: A Sourcebook of His Life and Writings*, ed. Homer A. Jack (New York: Grove/Atlantic, 1994), p. 312.

10. Arun Gandhi, "Nonviolence in Action," *SGI Quarterly*, July 2002, p. 10.

11. Daisaku Ikeda official website, < http://www.daisakuikeda.org/sub/resources/orks/props/ed-sustain2002.html >.

12. Emerson, "The Poet," in *Essays and Lectures*, p. 450.

13. Thoreau, *Walden*, in *A Week, Walden, The Maine Woods, Cape Cod*, p. 572.

Index

spiritual freedom and the,
29–30
spirituality of the, 32–34
American Revolution, 28, 29, 37
American Romanticism, 115–116,
151
Ananda, 53
Anglican Church, 27
antislavery movement, 3, 33, 40,
54–55, 116
Asian Tsunami, xxi, 149
Atlantic Monthly, 60
Augustine, Saint, 110
authoritarianism, 168

Bhâgavata Purâna, 67
Bhagvat Geeta, 160
Blake, Harrison Gray Otis, 62–63
Blake, William, 115
Bonaparte, Napoleon, 108, 109, 111
books, 63–66. *See also* reading
Bosco, Ronald, xix–xxv, 2, 22, 158,
164, 172, 174
on the American Renaissance,
26
childhood of, 7–8
early influences on, 9, 10–11
Emerson and, 15–17, 20, 21,
24, 83–85, 86, 126
The Emerson Brothers: A
Fraternal Biography in
Letters, 84, 86
Emerson-Thoreau studies and,
18–19, 20
The Later Lectures of Ralph
Waldo Emerson, 84
lecture at Soka University of
America, 36

Myerson and, 24
at Purdue University, 18
"Serving the Essential Needs
of Education," 145–146
at Soka University of America,
36, 131–132
at Soka University of Japan, 107
at State University of New
York at Albany, 19
Thoreau and, 15–17, 20, 21, 24
Thoreau Society and, 15,
23–24, 75
at University of Maryland, 18
Vietnam War and, 15–17
Whitman and, 125–126
Boston, Massachusetts, 54, 87
Boston Research Center for the
21st Century. *See* Ikeda
Center for Peace, Learning
and Dialogue
Brazil, 7
British Romanticism, 151
Brook Farm Institute of
Agriculture and Education,
85
Brown, John, 40, 54, 143
Bruccoli, Matt, 13
Bryce Canyon National Park, 157
Buddhism, 53, 93, 112, 125, 138,
144, 153, 163–164. *See*
also Nichiren, Nichiren
Buddhism
Buddha nature, 112, 120,
163–164
doctrine of dependent
origination, 116
Mahayana Buddhism, 31
nature and, 73, 101

Dewey, John, 84, 168
  The Child and the Curriculum,
    136
dialogue, 3, 172
  Socratic, 141
Dillard, Annie, 41
divinity, 77, 108, 153, 163–164

Earth Charter Initiative, 165
earthquake. *See* Great Sumatra-
    Andaman Islands
    Earthquake
Eastern Europe, democratization
    of, 6
Eastern literature, xx, 125
Eastern thought, 21, 60, 67–68,
    99, 101, 125, 160–161
East-West philosophical
    exchanges, 60
education, 6, 17–18, 33, 65, 94,
    113, 131, 139–147, 170. *See
    also* mentoring; service-
    learning movement
  Alcott on, 140–142
  challenges facing, 146
  Emerson and, 132–138, 139,
    146, 147
  environmental, 166, 169
  happiness and, 136, 138
  Ikeda on, 134–135, 136
  in Japan, 141
  lifelong learning, 142–143
  Makiguchi and, 135, 136, 140,
    142, 145
  nonviolence education, 169
  poetry and, 143–145
  practical experience, 165–168,
    171

self-culture, 76, 139–140
  Thoreau and, 139–147
  Toda and, 141
egoism, 113, 170
Ellison, Ralph, 10
Emerson, Charles (brother), 86,
    87, 92, 94
Emerson, Edward (brother), 86,
    87, 92, 94
Emerson, Edward Waldo (son),
    61, 160–161
Emerson, Ellen (daughter), 96
Emerson, Ellen Louisa Tucker
    (wife), 88, 91, 92, 94
Emerson, Mary Moody (aunt),
    61, 110
Emerson, Ralph Waldo, xx, xxii–
    xxiii, 2, 4–6, 12, 17, 19–20,
    24–25, 53, 61, 67, 83–90,
    116, 132, 168, 172, 174. *See
    also* Emerson, Ralph Waldo,
    works of
  American Renaissance and,
    84–85, 110–112
  appearance of, 44
  audience of, 91–97
  on the "balanced soul," 97
  books and, 63–64, 65
  in Boston, Massachusetts, 108
  careers of, 133
  Christianity and, 104–105
  on the Civil War, 120–121
  in Concord, Massachusetts, 96
  Concord lyceum and, 143
  on consistency, 108
  correspondence and, 101
  critical thinking and, 102–104
  death and, 91–92

death of, 96
declining health of, 96
on democracy, 84, 110, 121
on divinity, 108, 164
Eastern thought and, 32–33,
    99, 101, 160–161
on education, 132–136, 136–
    139, 146, 147
education of, 85–86
Ellen's death and, 91–92
Emerson studies, 18–21
environmental issues and, 156
family of, 85–87
first encounters of authors
    with, 15–24
funeral oration for Thoreau,
    46
at Harvard, 85–86, 87–88, 134
on humanity, 107–113
on individual reform, 84–85,
    112–113
industrialism and, 121
influence of, 69, 84
later years of, 96–97
leaves ministry, 90, 92, 93–94
library of, 63–64
literary nationalism and, 68
"little-endians," 109–110
on the Lord's Supper, 88, 89
lyceum movement and, 94, 144
Makiguchi and, 136–137
in Manchester, England, 108
on "Man Thinking," 103, 104
marriage to Ellen Louisa
    Tucker, 88
as mentor, xxiv
as minister, 87–90, 92, 93–94,
    133

Muir, John, and, 151, 157–159
on nature, 51, 99–102, 149–
    150, 153, 159, 160–162
optimism of, 111, 116
on originality, 103
in Paris, France, 101
peace movement and, 15–17
philosophy of, 99–102, 110–
    112, 132–135
Platonic and neo-Platonic
    thought and, 99
poetry and, 36, 127–128
poses difficult questions,
    93–94
publication of, 63, 95
reception in Japan, 68, 107
reexamination of life and,
    91–93
religion and, 87–90, 104–105
at Second Church of Boston,
    88, 90, 92
on social reform, 84–85,
    112–113
as teacher, 132–133
Thoreau and, 21–22, 41–46,
    55, 61, 69, 94, 168
Transcendent idealism and, 88
on translations, 68
ultimate goal of, 133–134
Unitarianism and, 88, 133
Walden Pond and, 74
Whitman and, 94–95, 126, 127,
    128–129
Emerson, Ralph Waldo, works of
    "The American Scholar," 29,
    30, 31, 43, 94, 102–104,
    106, 107, 133
    "Compensation," 91–92, 93

the Gospels, 67

Grand Canyon National Park, 157. *See also* national parks

Great Sumatra-Andaman Islands Earthquake, xxi

Green Belt Movement, 150–152. *See also* Maatthai, Wangari

Green Revolution, 169

Habbington, William, "To My Honoured Friend Sir Ed. P. Knight," 118

happiness, 136, 138

Harding, Walter, 64

Harvard College, 64, 85–86, 139

Harvard Divinity School, 87, 102, 104, 105

Harvard University, 83–84, 134. *See also* Harvard College

Hawthorne, Nathaniel, xxiii, 12, 53, 61, 110–111, 116, 143–144
religion and, 116–117
Scarlet Letter, 26

Hawthorne, Sophia, 143–144

Hawthorne family, 96

Hayford, Harrison, 13

health, 160, 162–163

Herbart, Johann Friedrich, 159

heroes, 109, 110–112

Hindu texts, 67

Hokkaido, Japan, 86

Hokkaido Normal School, 86

Holmes, Oliver Wendell, 31

Hong Kong, 7

Houghton Library, Harvard University, 83–84

Houghton Mifflin, 63

Hugo, Victor, 69–70

human development, 59–70

humanism, 31, 170

humanity, 172
geography and, 154
nature and, 150, 159, 161–162, 162–163, 170–172
ordinary people, 110
poetry and, 115–116
revitalization of, 107–108

human revolution, 34, 80–81, 112–113, 170

human rights, 27, 33, 165, 168, 171

human rights movement, 2, 16, 80, 170

Hurricane Katrina, 149–150

ignorance, 118–120

Ikeda, Daisaku, xix–xx, xxi, xxii–xxiii, xxiv, 2–3, 5, 92, 161–162, 172–174. *See also* Ikeda, Daisaku, works of
on the American Renaissance, 25–26
books and, 65–66
childhood of, 8–9
commencement message sent by, 132
early influences on, 9, 10–11
on education, 134–135, 136
Emerson and, xx, 12, 17–18, 19, 36, 83, 89, 93, 106, 116, 173
Emerson-Thoreau studies and, 19
founding of Soka University by, 35, 65, 146–147
Honorary Life Membership in the Thoreau Society, 1

on Hurricane Katrina, 149
imprisonment of, 79–80
lectures of, 89, 106
library of, 65
nature and, 72–73
peace movement and, 41
peace proposals of, 106, 108,
    113
photographs of, 72–73
on poetry, xxv, 116, 144–145
poetry of, xx, 144–145
on reading, 65–66, 68–69
Thoreau and, xx, 19, 36, 116
Toda and, 18, 21
Transcendentalism and, 106
Whitman and, xx, 19, 36, 116,
    123–124
World War II and, 17
Ikeda, Daisaku, works of
    "The Age of Soft Power,"
        17–18, 106
    "The Challenge of Global
        Empowerment," 170
    The Human Revolution, 17, 80
    Songs from My Heart, 116
    "The University of the 21st
        Century—Cradle of World
        Citizens," 132
Ikeda, Kaneko, xix
Ikeda, Ki'ichi, 17
Ikeda Center for Peace, Learning
    and Dialogue, vii, xx, 22,
    59–60, 173
Ikeda Forum for Intercultural
    Dialogue, 59–60, 173
imaginative freedom, 28
independence, 27–28, 29. *See also*
    freedom; *specific freedoms*

India, 7
Indians (American). *See*
    American Indians
individual, nature and, 50–52
individualism, xx, 12, 166, 173
individual reform, 84–85, 112–113
industrialization, 4, 25, 34, 121,
    170
industrialized nations, 171
industrial revolution, 34, 170
Institutes of Hindu Law, 67
intellectual freedom, 27–28. *See
    also* American intellectual
    independence

James, William, 167
Japan, 79, 152. *See also specific
    cities*
    education in, 141 (*see also* Soka
        education)
    environmental issues in, 1
    fascism in, 6
    reading in, 69
    reception of Emerson in, 68,
        107
    reception of Thoreau in, 1, 21
    religious freedom in, 27–28
    students in, 5
Japanese philosophy, 21. *See also*
    Eastern thought
Jardin des Plantes, 101
Jishu Gakkan, 141
Jones, William, 67

Kamo no Chomei, *Hojoki*
    ("Account of My Hut"), 49
Keats, John, 115
Kennedy, John F., 16

Shakyamuni Buddha, 30, 53, 67, 74, 93, 110
Shelly, Percy Byssche, 115
Shinto, 27
Sierra Club, 151
Singapore, 7
skepticism, 115
slavery, 40. *See also* antislavery movement
Sleepy Hollow Cemetery, 96
social justice, 4, 77, 84–85
social movements, 22
social reform, 34, 84–85, 112–113
Socrates, 60, 93, 110
Socratic dialogue, 141
Soka community, xxi
Soka education, xxiii, 135, 136, 138, 141, 146–147. *See also* Soka schools; Soka University
Soka Gakkai International, xix, xx, 6, 18, 27, 80, 93, 106, 107, 144, 153, 165, 171
   activism of, 170
   American Renaissance and, 90
   Buddhism and, 89
   charter of, 32–34
   culture movement of, 113
   education movement of, 113
   Emerson and, 32–34
   faith and, 89–90
   human revolution and, 112, 170
   ideals of, 172
   peace movement of, 113
   Thoreau and, 32–34
Soka schools, xix, 5, 22, 146–147. *See also* Soka education; Soka University

Soka University
   of America, xix, xxi, xxii, 5, 35–36, 65, 131, 141, 146–147, 157, 172
   of Japan, xix, 2, 5, 19, 65, 146–147, 172
the South, 28
Sparks, Jared, 64
spirituality, 26, 32–34
   spiritual freedom, 29, 30
   spiritual revolution, 34
the State, 78
Sumatra, 149
Swaminathan, M. S., 169
Swedenborg, Emanuel, 108
Swift, Jonathan, *Gulliver's Travels*, 109–110

teaching, 132–133, 137–138, 139–140. *See also* education; lecturing
technology, 32, 34, 170
temperance, 116
theocracy, 27–28
Thoreau, Henry David, xx, xxii–xxiii, xxv–xxvi, 1–13, 17, 20, 24–25, 29–31, 94, 110, 113, 116, 132, 174. *See also* Thoreau, Henry David, works of
   abolitionism of, 40–41, 54–55
   Alcott and, 141–142
   American Indians and, 56–58
   appearance of, 44
   art of conversation and, 172
   on authoritarianism, 168
   books and, 63–64, 65–66
   changing views of, 3–4

About the Authors

RONALD A. BOSCO is Distinguished Professor of English and American Literature at the University at Albany, State University of New York, and general editor for *The Collected Works of Ralph Waldo Emerson* (Harvard University Press). A past president of the Thoreau Society and the Ralph Waldo Emerson Society, Professor Bosco also lectures on the influence of Calvinist thought in American culture. His recent collaboration with Joel Myerson, *The Emerson Brothers: A Fraternal Biography in Letters*, was published by Oxford University Press in 2006.

JOEL MYERSON is Carolina Distinguished Professor of American Literature, Emeritus, at the University of South Carolina, and textual editor for *The Collected Works of Ralph Waldo Emerson* (Harvard University Press). Professor Myerson has served as president of several organizations preserving the legacy of the American Renaissance, including the Thoreau Society, the Ralph Waldo Emerson Society, the Margaret Fuller Society, and the Louisa May Alcott Society. Among his many collaborations with Ronald A. Bosco is *The Selected Lectures of Ralph Waldo Emerson*, published by the University of Georgia Press in 2005.

DAISAKU IKEDA is President of Soka Gakkai International, a lay Buddhist organization with more than 12 million members worldwide. He has written and lectured widely on Buddhism, humanism, and global ethics. More than 50 of his dialogues have been published in book form, including conversations with figures such as Mikhail Gorbachev, Hazel Henderson, Joseph Rotblat, Linus Pauling, and Arnold Toynbee. Dedicated to education promoting humanistic ideals, in 1971 President Ikeda founded Soka University in Tokyo, and, in 2001, Soka University America in Alisa Viejo, California.